STRUGGLE AND LOVE

WITH
Jesse
JOBS NOW
JOBS
PEACE
FREEDOM
JOBS
NOT
BOMBS
JOBS
NOT
BOMBS

MILESTONES IN BLACK AMERICAN HISTORY

STRUGGLE AND LOVE

1972-1997

FROM THE GARY CONVENTION
TO THE AFTERMATH
OF THE MILLION MAN MARCH

Mary Hull

CHELSEA HOUSE PUBLISHERS
Philadelphia

ON THE COVER: Clasped hands at the Million Man March reflect the unity, despite inherent differences, of African Americans as they face the struggles of the late 1990s.

FRONTISPIECE: Jesse Jackson protests President Ronald Reagan's second term on Inauguration Day, 1985. The slogans on the protesters' signs illustrate that Jackson's political concerns are not strictly "black" issues—as would be the case for many African Americans entering politics after the 1970s.

Chelsea House Publishers

Editorial Director	Richard Rennert
Production Manager	Pamela Loos
Art Director	Sara Davis
Picture Editor	Judy Hasday

Milestones in Black American History

Series Originator and Adviser	Benjamin I. Cohen
Series Consultants	Clayborne Carson, Darlene Clark Hine

Staff for STRUGGLE AND LOVE

Senior Editor	Jane Shumate
Associate Editor	Therese De Angelis
Editorial Assistant	Kristine Brennan
Designer	Alison Burnside
Picture Researcher	Patricia Burns

First Printing
1 3 5 7 9 8 6 4 2

Library of Congress Cataloging-in-Publication Data

Hull, Mary.
Struggle and love: from the Gary Convention to the present (1972-) / Mary Hull.
p. cm.—(Milestones in Black American history)
Includes bibliographical references (p.) and index.
Summary: Discusses the efforts of African Americans to achieve equality in education, employment, politics, and other areas, from the 1970s into the 1990s.
ISBN 0-7910-2262-5 (hc)
0-7910-2688-4 (pbk)
1. Afro-Americans—Civil rights—Juvenile literature. 2. Civil rights movements—United States—History—20th century—Juvenile literature. 3. Afro-Americans—History—1964—Juvenile literature. [1. Afro-Americans—Civil rights. 2. Afro-Americans—Social conditions —1975-] I. Title. II. Series.
E185.615.H85 1996 96-30513
973'.0496073—dc20 CIP
AC

CONTENTS

MILESTONES IN BLACK AMERICAN HISTORY

Ancient Egypt, Ethiopia, and Nubia

The West African Kingdoms (750-1900)

The Age of Discovery and the Slave Trade

From the Arrival of the Enslaved Africans
to the End of the American Revolution (1619-1784)

From the Framing of the Constitution
to *Walker's Appeal* (1787-1829)

From the Nat Turner Revolt
to the Fugitive Slave Law (1831-1850)

From Uncle Tom's Cabin
to the Onset of the Civil War (1851-1861)

From the Emancipation Proclamation
to the Civil Rights Bill of 1875 (1863-1875)

From the End of Reconstruction
to the Atlanta Compromise (1877-1895)

From the "Separate but Equal" Doctrine
to the Birth of the NAACP (1896-1909)

From the Great Migration
to the Harlem Renaissance (1910-1930)

From the Scottsboro Case
to the Breaking of Baseball's Color Barrier (1931-1947)

From the Desegregation of the Armed Forces
to the Montgomery Bus Boycott (1948-1956)

From the Founding of the Southern Christian
Leadership Conference to the Assassination of Malcolm X
(1957-1965)

From the Selma-Montgomery March
to the Formation of PUSH (1965-1971)

From the Gary Convention
to the Aftermath of the Million Man March (1972-1997)

INTRODUCTION

✵

The period from 1972 to the present has been a struggle for leadership and focus among African Americans; it has been a struggle both to build consensus and to accept the diversity of black politics. A steady stream of congressional actions, executive orders, and federal court decisions had achieved tremendous legal and civil rights victories in the 1950s and 1960s. But, by 1972, the movement appeared to have lost its momentum: black Americans were not enjoying much economic improvement, and much of the movement toward legal and political improvements had stalled. Under the slogan of "Unity Without Uniformity," black political, civil rights, and community organizers met at the Gary Convention in 1972 in an unprecedented attempt to unite black leadership and build a black political organization that could carry out the vision of the civil rights movement of the previous decades.

In the years since the Gary Convention there has been a noticeable increase in black political and economic empowerment. African Americans began filling the nation's political parties and elected positions; with Shirley Chisholm's candidacy in 1972 and Jesse Jackson's campaigns in 1984 and 1988, African Americans entered the realm of presidential politics. Segregation in northern classrooms—which had continued quietly despite forced changes in the South—was confronted in the 1970s, as federally mandated busing sparked controversy around the country. And the nation's courtrooms became a battleground for the policies of affirmative action, which have given more African Americans access to higher education and employment opportunities.

After Gary, the development of the black consciousness movement in the early 1970s led to a revolution in the nation's universities and to a wealth of new images of African Americans in cultural media, from sound waves to print. The outrage of black America was heard, too: in Miami and Los Angeles especially, African Americans resorted to rioting in order to make their voices heard when juries failed to convict police accused of brutality against minorities. Their rioting forced the nation to pay attention to the serious economic and social problems of its urban areas.

Finally, responding to the declining quality of black neighborhoods and the growing crisis of survival faced by black men in the 1990s, organizers of the Million Man March sought to focus attention on problems within the black community and instill a sense of communal mission in black men. The march motivated a whole new generation of activists to work to rebuild black neighborhoods, and it stirred new determination to tackle the problems facing African Americans, strengthening the will to continue the struggle into the next century.

MILESTONES
1972-1997

1972 January: Congresswoman Shirley Chisholm announces her bid for the presidency.

March: Eight thousand delegates gather in Gary, Indiana, for the First National Black Political Convention. They develop a National Black Political Agenda designed to further the major concerns of black Americans in 1972.

1973 October: Maynard Jackson is elected the first African-American mayor of Atlanta, Georgia, and begins an aggressive affirmative action campaign to employ minority contractors in the construction of the Atlanta airport.

1974 April: Henry "Hank" Aaron of the Atlanta Braves breaks Babe Ruth's record for the most career home runs.

June: Judge Arthur Garrity, ruling that Boston's public school system is "unconstitutionally segregated," orders a desegregation plan that involves mandatory busing of students. The busing program, which begins in September, sparks demonstrations and violence.

Frank Robinson, the only man in history to be named the Most Valuable Player in both the American and National leagues, is appointed manager of the Cleveland Indians: the first African American to achieve this rank in baseball.

1975 January: Muhammad Ali edges out Hank Aaron to become the Associated Press's athlete of the year.

1976 October: The last of the Scottsboro Boys, Clarence "Willie" Norris, is pardoned for a faulty rape conviction in 1931.

November: Unita Blackwell, a founding member of the Mississippi Freedom Democratic Party, is the first black woman mayor elected in the history of Mississippi.

1977 April: Alex Haley wins a special Pulitzer Prize for *Roots*, which sells 1.6 million copies in its first six months in print and is translated into 22 languages. The television miniseries adapted from the book engrosses 130 million Americans and sweeps the Emmy Awards.

October: Reggie Jackson of the New York Yankees becomes the first baseball player to hit three home runs in a World Series game. Jackson leads the Yankees to a Series victory over the Los Angeles Dodgers, earning him the nickname "Mr. October."

1978 June: The Supreme Court rules in *Regents v. Bakke* that the University of California's affirmative action policies are the equivalent of reverse discrimination, and Alan Bakke is admitted to U.C. Davis. The court also rules that race may be considered as one factor in selecting candidates for admission.

1980 The Sugar Hill Gang releases *Rapper's Delight*, the first rap record with national airplay, marking the debut of a new musical genre that will become a national phenomenon over the next decade.

May: Eighteen people die in three days of racial rioting in Miami that began to protest the acquittal of police officers charged with excessive force.

1981 Basketball star "Magic" Johnson signs a 25-year, $25-million contract with the Los Angeles Lakers, the largest total sum in sports team history.

1982 Michael Jackson releases *Thriller*, which becomes the best-selling album of all time, with over 40 million copies sold.

1983 November: Following a massive voter-registration campaign, Harold Washington is elected the first black mayor of Chicago.

1984 November: Jesse Jackson garners 300 delegates for the Democratic National Convention in his first bid for the presidency.

1985 "We Are the World," written by Michael Jackson and Lionel Richie, produced by Quincy Jones, and sung by the largest gathering of musical celebrities in history, is released. Proceeds benefit African famine-relief efforts.

1986 December: Michael Griffith is murdered by three white men in a racially motivated attack in the Howard Beach section of Queens, New York.

1988 August: Approximately 55,000 Americans gather at the Mall in Washington to commemorate the 25th anniversary of the March on Washington.

Jesse Jackson places second in the Democratic presidential primary, losing to Massachusetts governor Michael Dukakis.

1989 January: In the most far-reaching criticism of affirmative action since the 1978 *Bakke* decision, the Supreme Court rules against a minority set-aside program in Virginia, claiming it is unconstitutional and an unlawful form of reverse discrimination.

June: The Supreme Court rules that workers who are "adversely affected by court-approved affirmative action plans may file law suits alleging discrimination."

August: Yusuf Hawkins is killed by white youths in Bensonhurst, New York. The racially motivated killing prompts a march by thousands of protesters.

Four-star general Colin Powell is named chairman of the U.S. Joint Chiefs of Staff, the highest military position in the country. At 52, Powell is the youngest man and the first African American to lead the joint chiefs.

1990 January: Douglas Wilder of Virginia becomes the nation's first black governor.

October: President George Bush vetoes the Civil Rights Bill of 1990, saying that the document "employs a maze of highly legalistic language to introduce the destructive force of quotas" into the workplace.

1991 January: The U.S. goes to war with Iraq. Of the 400,000 U.S. troops in the Persian Gulf, 104,400 are African American. General Colin Powell calls the U.S. military "the greatest equal opportunity employer around."

March: Rodney King is beaten by several white Los Angeles police officers who stopped him for speeding.

October: After controversial hearings during which Anita Hill accuses him of sexual harassment, Clarence Thomas is confirmed to the Supreme Court.

November: "Magic" Johnson's announcement that he is retiring from the National Basketball Association after testing positive for HIV focuses attention on the disease.

December: A group of black teenagers who were denied service at a Denny's Restaurant in California bring a successful lawsuit against the restaurant chain.

1992

April: The four Los Angeles police officers accused of beating motorist Rodney King are acquitted, prompting rioting in South Central Los Angeles that will continue for four days and become the worst urban uprising in three decades.

August: Jackie Joyner-Kersee becomes the first woman to repeat as Olympic Heptathlon champion at the Summer Olympics in Barcelona.

Ron Brown chairs the Democratic National Convention in New York City, where, for the first time, African Americans dominate administrative roles.

1993

Author Toni Morrison wins a Nobel Prize for literature for a body of work that includes the Pulitzer Prize–winning *Beloved.*

January: For the first time, all 50 states (including long-time holdouts Arizona and New Hampshire) observe Martin Luther King Day.

May: Rita Dove becomes the first black woman to serve as U.S. Poet Laureate; in 1985 she won the Pulitzer Prize for *Thomas and Beaulah,* a collection of poetry inspired by her grandparents.

1994

June: Former football star O. J. Simpson is accused of murdering his former wife, Nicole Brown Simpson, and her friend Ronald Goldman, setting off a media sensation.

1995

October: After being sequestered for 266 days, a California jury finds O. J. Simpson not guilty of murdering Nicole Brown Simpson and Ronald Goldman.

The Million Man March, headed by the Nation of Islam's Louis Farrakhan and Dr. Benjamin Chavis, is held in Washington, evoking a national response and call to action within African-American communities.

1996

April: Secretary of Commerce Ron Brown, with a delegation of U.S. business leaders, dies in an airplane crash over Croatia while on a mission to promote U.S. trade.

WEST VIRGINIA
WYOMING

1

"UNITY WITHOUT UNIFORMITY"

African-American history has been described as the history of the struggle between integrationist and nationalist forces in politics, culture, and economics. Integrationists choose to eliminate differences between themselves and white citizens, while nationalists choose to retain and even elevate their differences as black people: but both share the goal of black political power. Although integrationists believe that they must work within the existing political and economic power structure—doing so often by gaining elected office—nationalists feel that they can only work outside it.

Yet Martin Luther King, Jr., who came to lead the integrationist civil rights movement, and Malcolm X, one of the foremost black nationalist leaders, both had a vision at the end of their lives of a universal movement for civil rights, unhindered by different politics or religion. In his "Black Revolution" speech, Malcolm X talked about the idea of nationalists and integrationists coming together: "Our people have made the mistake of confusing the methods with the

Jesse Jackson speaks at the Gary Convention, where 8,000 African Americans gathered to formulate a new black political agenda. "We are 25 million strong," he exclaimed. "Cut us in or cut us out!"

objectives. As long as we agree on objectives, we should never fall out with each other just because we believe in different methods or tactics or strategy to reach a common objective."

Under the theme of "Unity Without Uniformity," 8,000 African Americans representing the spectrum of black political and social thought traveled to Gary, Indiana, in March 1972 to listen to one another and attempt to find common ground. This all-black political assembly had been endorsed by integrationists and nationalists alike, and their arrival in Gary would give the impression that a new union of forces had begun for black leadership in America.

"To drive into Gary, Indiana, and see streamers red, black, and green, and 'Welcome National Black Political Convention' . . . was a fulfillment of what a lot of our dreams were." So recalled Benjamin Chavis, one of the thousands of African Americans who traveled from all over the nation to attend the first National Black Political Convention. According to Chavis, at that time African Americans had grown so disillusioned with the United States under President Richard M. Nixon that to receive this welcome in Gary made them believe they "were in a different country."

Of the 8,000, some 3,300 were delegates representing a variety of civil rights, community, and political organizations. They came to Gary—to what would be known as the Gary Convention—in an unprecedented attempt to unite black leadership and build a black political organization that could carry out the vision of the civil rights movement, setting priorities for black Americans and mobilizing support for black public policy initiatives. Gary had been selected as the site for the National Black Political Convention because its new mayor, Richard Hatcher, was one of the first African Americans elected to lead a large U.S. city.

Dr. Martin Luther King, Jr., and Malcolm X greet each other at the Capitol in 1964. Although the integrationist Dr. King and the nationalist Malcolm X embodied the rift between the two prevailing forces in black politics, both came to a similar vision of unity by the end of their lives.

The idea of a convention was not a new one for black Americans. In 1830, Richard Allen, the founder of the African Methodist Episcopal Church, organized the first national black convention, the American Society of Free Persons of Colour, at Bethel Church in Philadelphia. Seventy-five years later, W. E. B. Du Bois organized a convention "of men who believe in Negro freedom and growth"; held in Fort Erie, Ontario, close to Niagara Falls, it gave rise to the Niagara Movement, whose membership consisted of a select group of influential blacks. But the Gary Convention was the most significant contemporary attempt to build a national black political organization, and it represented a shift from the protest tactics of the 1960s—marches, sit-ins, and freedom rides—to political strategy.

Black attempts to work with either Democrats or Republicans—the two national political parties—had left them feeling they had been sold out, their support taken with little given back, and the promises made to them unkept or fulfilled only after intense pressure. Indeed, from the Hayes-Tilden compromise of 1877—which removed federal troops from the South and left blacks at the mercy of their former masters—to the failure of President Franklin D. Roosevelt to desegregate the armed forces, to President John F. Kennedy's stalling on the long-promised "stroke of the pen" that would end discrimination in federally financed housing, politicians had consistently failed to deliver on promises made to their African-American voters. The reality was that not even the "heroes" of black Americans—Abraham Lincoln or Roosevelt or Kennedy—had ever moved on behalf of black people without tremendous pressure.

After the election of Nixon as president in 1968, many black Americans felt even more strongly the repression of black activism. They were ready to form their own institutions. Although earlier attempts at forming a black third party had been made—most notably the 1960 Afro-American party movement in the South, the 1964 Freedom Now Northern Party, and the 1964 Mississippi Freedom Democratic Party (MFDP)—none of these parties had taken root.

In the 1968 publication *Black Power*, political activists Stokely Carmichael and Charles Hamilton had theorized that "a viable coalition cannot exist between the politically and economically secure and the politically and economically insecure." The Black Power movement that emerged in the late 1960s among young people who had grown up in organizations like the Student Non-Violent Coordinating Committee (SNCC) and the Congress of Racial Equality (CORE) consequently encouraged black Americans to rely on one another for economic and political power. Slogans like "Black Power for Black People" and "Black Is Beautiful" spread the ideas of black control over community institutions and pride in black culture, physiognomy, and history.

By 1972, African Americans were fully ready to think about starting their own political organization—one that would unite disparate elements of black leadership in an attempt to gain political efficacy. With this hope, black Americans came to the Gary Convention.

Black elected officials and black nationalists, who rarely saw eye to eye, had worked together in a new spirit of cooperation to organize the convention. Amiri Baraka of the Congress of African Peoples, U.S. Representative Charles Diggs of Michigan, and Gary mayor Richard Hatcher had called the convention. Their shared hope was to convert black political potential into black political power.

"It was an enormously exciting experiment and idea," recalled black entertainer and activist Harry Belafonte. "Could we come together, this diverse group? And in the absence of the glue that had held it together previously—meaning Dr. King, meaning Malcolm X—in the absence of those leaders . . . [c]ould there be a consensus?"

Indeed the 3,300 delegates represented a variety of political views, from radical to conservative. Among the delegates at Gary were Bobby Seale, the cofounder of the militant Black Panther Party; Samuel C. Jackson, assistant secretary of Housing and Urban Development in the Nixon administration;

The assassination of Martin Luther King, Jr., by a white sniper threatened to extinguish the civil rights movement. King's widow, Coretta Scott King, leads a memorial march through Memphis, Tennessee, with her children Yolanda, Martin III, and Dexter. Harry Belafonte is on the far left.

Jesse Jackson, founder of Operation PUSH (People United to Save Humanity); Betty Shabazz, widow of Malcolm X, the former Black Muslim and founder of the Organization of Afro-American Unity (OAU); Amiri Baraka and Queen Mother Moore of the Congress of African Peoples; Charles Diggs and other members of the Congressional Black Caucus; and Coretta Scott King, widow of Martin Luther King, Jr., of the Southern Christian Leadership Conference (SCLC).

The convention was the most ideologically and physically diverse assembly that Gary mayor Richard Hatcher had ever seen, but he was excited by the disparate makeup of people. "It was probably one of the most glorious moments of my life," he recalled, "when I looked out and saw all of these black people of every color . . . [t]he colorful dashikis and other African garb that some of them wore, mixing with three-piece suits and so forth. It was just an incredible sight to behold."

Although diverse in appearance, background, and political affiliation, what the delegates at Gary shared was frustration and anger over their exclusion from the political process and the loss of political leadership with the murders of King, Malcolm X, and John and Robert Kennedy. In his speech before the thousands of delegates, Jesse Jackson expressed this sense of urgency and frustration: "We are pregnant! We are ready for change, and whether a doctor is there or not, the water has broke, the blood has spilled—a new black baby is gonna be born! . . . No more bowing and scraping! We are 25 million strong. Cut us in or cut us out!" And when Jackson asked the assembled crowd, "When we come together, what time is it?" the crowd swelled with the response: "Nation time!"

Sitting in groups near signs bearing the names of their home states, the delegates deliberated for three days, with talks revolving around an "outline for a black agenda," a rough draft that had been prepared by a task force before the convention. Beginning with the premise that "the American system does not work for the masses of our people and it cannot be made to work without radical fundamental change," the outline contained 30 steps to eliminate racism and exploitation from American life, and it called on blacks to organize in order to realize these goals. On the floor of the convention hall, delegates stood to propose resolutions to problems faced by their constituencies, as well as larger problems faced by all Americans. Addressed were goals such as improved education for black children, political empowerment, rural development, employment, national health insurance, day care, elder care, foreign policy, and environmental protection.

But with all the conflicting ideologies present, it was not easy to reach a consensus. And on the last day of the convention, as delegates were finally voting to adopt the resolutions that had been proposed into the National Black Political Agenda, the conflict between black nationalists and black elected officials came to a dramatic head. Coleman Young, mayor of Detroit, walked out under criticism that the Michigan delegation was unresponsive to black grassroots interests. Michigan, the majority of whose delegates represented auto and steel workers, feared that the separatist tone of the agenda would jeopardize black alliances with organized labor. With moderator Amiri Baraka trying to keep everything from flying apart, the crowd was tense with the fear that if Michigan walked out, other groups would soon follow. But some of the Michigan delegation stayed, proclaiming there was no interest strong enough to overpower black unity.

The crowd became jubilant as the document called "Action Agenda for Black People" was ratified. The delegates shouted and cheered, waving their signs. The convention closed triumphantly to the cry "It's nation time! Let the black nation rise!"

The 55-page "Action Agenda" that came out of the Gary Convention reflected the major concerns of the cross section of black Americans represented there in 1972, and it laid out strategies for achieving political and economic empowerment, increased black control over community institutions, and increased black input into national and foreign policy making. The agenda declared,

> We come to Gary in an hour of great crisis and tremendous promise for black America. While the white nation hovers on the brink of chaos, while its politicians offer no hope of

Jesse Jackson at the Gary Convention. Jackson had fought alongside Dr. Martin Luther King, Jr., in the battle for civil rights and went on to found People United to Save Humanity (PUSH).

real change, we stand on the edge of history and are faced with an amazing and frightening choice: We may choose in 1972 to slip back into the decadent white politics of American life, or we may press forward, moving relentlessly from Gary to the creation of our own Black life.

The agenda ended with a hopeful declaration: "This is our challenge at Gary and beyond, for a new black politics demands new vision, new hope, and

United in spirit, divided by issues: despite this show of solidarity, tensions between nationalists and elected officials at the Gary Convention ran high.

new definition of the possible. Our time has come. These things are necessary. All things are possible."

Although the display of unity at the Gary Convention was impressive, there was much disagreement over the provisions of the black agenda, which would ultimately lead to its disintegration. The National Association for the Advancement of Colored People (NAACP), for example, withdrew its support because it objected to the agenda's description of school busing to achieve desegregation as "sui-

cidal" and "racist," and it disapproved of the agenda's call for the "dismantling" of Israel and its "expansionist" policy. Furthermore, although the Gary Convention established a continuing national structure called the National Black Political Assembly, this too lasted only a short time: as early as 1974, it had become dominated by community activists, progressive intellectuals, grass-roots leaders, and nationalists—and had only a few black elected officials representing the integrationist sector. Although this assembly continued to meet biannually, differences among its diverse members ultimately led to its demise.

Thus, the very mandate that created the Gary Convention and its agenda was also, paradoxically, its downfall: "unity without uniformity." This coming together despite differences was the only thing that could make the coalition possible, but it also made the coalition impossible. Scholars view the agenda at the Gary Convention as a fleeting compromise between the incompatible views of black nationalists and black integrationists, between the advocates of an independent black political party and those committed to the two-party system—the age-old conflict between revolutionaries and reformists. While these diverse groups were able to unite behind a common declaration, this unity was shattered once the groups tried to build structures to implement their goals.

According to professors of African-American political history Lucius Barker and Mack Jones, the backgrounds of the different groups at the Gary Convention compromised their ability to pursue certain agendas. For example, most of the elected officials at the Gary Convention were members of the Democratic party; they were therefore reluctant to form an independent black political party. Because the agenda's foreign policy favored Arabs over Israelis in the Middle East, members of the Congressional Black Caucus could not endorse it without risking the financial support of their Jewish constituencies.

The problems of building a broad coalition of interests continue to confront the black community today. In the absence of a national black political organization, African Americans have continued to look to the Republican and Democratic parties to find political empowerment, and they have filled these parties with their own ranks. In the words of Richard Hatcher, "People went back home, rolled up their sleeves, and ran for public office in a way that blacks had never thought about running for public office before." At the same time, however, separatism has retained a potent appeal and has continued to find powerful representation through such organizations as the Nation of Islam and its leader, Louis Farrakhan.

The "Action Agenda" formed in Gary in 1972 declared that "all things are possible." Not only would African Americans thereafter enter the political arena in unprecedented numbers; they would also demand that the integration of schools so painfully enacted in the South likewise be won in the North; they would pursue and defend the job and educational opportunities held out by affirmative action policies; they would transform American arts, studies, media, and sports; and they would resist with word and force the racial injustices lingering in the nation's legal system. In the quarter of a century that has followed the Gary Convention, African Americans have begun, as the "Action Agenda" put it, to move "relentlessly from Gary to the creation of our own Black life."

SCHOOL BUS
SCHOOL BUS
POLICE

2

MIXING SOUTHIE AND ROXBURY

Of the many issues that faced African Americans at the time of the Gary Convention, none was more explosive than the one involving education. "We are still a racist society," remarked columnist Carl Rowan nearly 20 years after the landmark 1954 *Brown v. Board of Education* U.S. Supreme Court ruling to desegregate public education in America. "Some of the litigants in that 1954 decision never saw a day of desegregated education. They saw evasion, circumvention, massive resistance, and a generation of litigation."

In the 1970s, public schools in the North were more segregated than those in the South. Unlike the Jim Crow laws that had segregated southern facilities, segregation in northern schools was a result of housing patterns: blacks and whites tended to live in different neighborhoods, and school districts were drawn along neighborhood lines. However, the Fourteenth Amendment to the Constitution had stated that separate schools were inherently unequal. As

Black students being bused home to Roxbury from South Boston as forced integration begins in the fall of 1974. The disturbing spectacle of a school bus behind a phalanx of police motorcycles soon became familiar.

Justice Earl Warren had written in the *Brown v. Board of Education* ruling,

> Segregation of white and colored children in public schools has a detrimental effect upon the colored children . . . it generates a feeling of inferiority as to their status in the community that may affect their hearts and minds in a way never to be undone . . . the doctrine of 'separate but equal' has no place in American public schools.

To desegregate schools in areas where housing patterns were accountable for the problem, busing of children between predominantly white or black schools had been ordered. Civil rights groups were divided over the issue of busing: while the NAACP supported busing to achieve desegregation, some members of CORE advocated separate "but really equal" schools under the control of the black community. A 1972 public-opinion poll found that 50 percent of blacks but only 14 percent of whites endorsed busing to achieve school desegregation. The controversy was to find its fullest expression in Boston in 1974.

As early as 1963, concerned black parents in Boston had complained to the Boston School Committee about the lack of educational opportunities for black students in the city's schools. Public schools in black neighborhoods received less funding than schools in white neighborhoods, and, as a result, the black schools were older and more dilapidated; there were shortages of textbooks, paper, and pencils; even desks and classrooms were scarce. Children who did not have desks had to sit in chairs beside the teacher's desk. In some schools, space was so limited that classes had to meet in gymnasiums.

In 1965, Boston parents had raised funds for a voluntary busing program known as Operation Exodus. But black students bused to predominantly white schools under this program found locked doors and classrooms where spare desks had been unbolted from the floor and removed. Rather than allow black students into neighboring white schools with extra space, the School Committee proposed to buy another school building for black students.

After more than a decade of struggling with the Boston School Committee, a group of black parents finally filed a class-action suit in federal court. In 1974, U.S. District Court judge W. Arthur Garrity ruled that the Boston public school system was "unconstitutionally segregated"—that it was violating the Fourteenth Amendment. While the School Committee maintained that any segregation was based on housing patterns, the judge ruled that the practices of the School Committee perpetuated the segregated system. The Boston School Committee was found guilty of practicing segregation in building new schools, changing district lines, setting up feeder patterns for high schools, and managing transfer and open-enrollment programs.

To racially balance the schools, Judge Garrity ordered the busing of several thousand pupils between the mostly black community of Roxbury and the mostly white communities of South Boston, Hyde Park, and Dorchester in the fall of 1974. The order prohibited the enrollment of 50 percent or more nonwhites in any school.

The busing order was a bombshell for many people in the white community. Whites who opposed busing staged demonstrations and boycotts reminiscent of the vehement opposition with which integration was met in the South in the 1950s and 1960s. Many white parents did not want their children to be bused into black communities, while others—associating blacks with crime—did not want black children brought to their neighborhood schools. The neighborhoods most affected were those of working-class

whites, and parents there were further angered that white upper-middle-class suburban neighborhoods were exempt from busing.

In his book *Liberty's Chosen Home: The Politics of Violence in Boston*, Alan Lupo expressed the collective fear of Boston's white working-class neighborhoods: "We are not very well off, but they [blacks] are worse off. If they come here, then we will be worse off. They must not come here and we must unite to

Making their objections clear on their signs, working-class parents protest forced busing outside a posh Boston hotel as Senator Edward Kennedy—one of busing's leading proponents—attends a fund-raising dinner inside.

make sure of that."

Just three days before the busing was scheduled to begin, an angry mob of antibusing demonstrators, most of them white women, heckled the pro-busing senator Ted Kennedy, splattering him with tomatoes as he tried to speak to the crowd that had gathered in Government Center. The demonstrators then marched to Judge Garrity's office, chanting, "Garrity must go!" Judge Garrity, who lived in the suburbs, was accused of elitism in his decision, which forced city neighborhoods, but not suburban ones, to integrate.

Before busing began, people from the mayor's office, the Office of Public Service, the Youth Activities Commission, and the school and police departments set up headquarters in the basement of Boston City Hall. A switchboard, phones, and police radios kept information flowing in and out of the headquarters. A network of community leaders for each neighborhood, from local fire and police chiefs to black and white community workers and youth group leaders, addressed safety concerns and worked to relay information about the busing to parents and students. As the first day of school approached, the sides were drawn: those who would put the desegregation plan in place and those who would resist it.

On the eve of the scheduled desegregation, Boston school superintendent William Leary said that, although everything possible had been done in the time allowed to prepare for desegregation, he knew there would be problems. Boston mayor Kevin White appealed for calm and warned that those who resorted to violence would be punished severely.

Finally, on September 12, 1974, the court-ordered integration of Boston public schools began. Many parents, both black and white, kept their children home on the first day of school, fearing for their safety. Some white parents refused to send their children to school on the premise that if no children were in school, there could be no desegregation. White students threw rocks at some of the school buses carrying black students, and black children transported to South Boston, Hyde Park, and Dorchester were met by jeering white parents who gathered outside the schools. Police on horseback were present as black children got off motorcycle-escorted buses in the white neighborhoods of South Boston.

The enforced order outside South Boston High School stopped at the door. Just two months after this picture was taken, a white student was stabbed in a fight. The incident placed all the black students at South Boston High in danger.

During the first week of busing, a crowd of white teenagers and mothers clashed with police officers outside South Boston High School. The police arrested 22 people and ordered the closing of bars and liquor stores in the area for the next two days. Violence and intense hostilities continued for several weeks: the slogan "Kill Niggers" appeared on buildings, and Nazi party members arrived in Boston, stirring up sympathy among those who protested Judge Garrity's order, passing out antiblack literature, and marching with signs that read "White Power."

Jean Louis Andre, a Haitian immigrant, is attacked by whites after being chased from his car in South Boston. He had driven there to pick up his daughter from school.

Thomas Atkins, Massachusetts Secretary for Communities and Development and also the informal spokesperson for the black community on the school case, received a warning from an anonymous informant that "all hell was going to break loose" if black students showed up for school at South Boston High the following day. The next morning, Atkins intercepted the students at their bus stops before they boarded for South Boston; meanwhile, a crowd of 1,500 to 2,000 people was waiting for them to arrive. When it became apparent that the buses were not going to show up, the crowd grew restless and began to split up. Some members of the crowd saw a black man alone in a car at a nearby stoplight and attacked his car. The man—a Haitian who had come to the neighborhood to fetch his daughter from school—fled his car and ran to a house for safety, but no one would let him in. Trapped, he was beaten with bottles and sticks.

This assault was just one example of the racial tension that existed during the first months of desegregation. Indeed, there was so much tension in the newly integrated schools that the slightest incident could spark a confrontation. Black and white students simply bumping into each other in the hallway could lead to a fight; at South Boston High, there were as many as 15 fights a day. One of the 56 black students assigned there described the environment:

> The black students sat on one side of the classes. The white students sat on the other side of the classes. The teachers didn't want to assign seating because there might be some problems in the classrooms. So the teachers basically let the students sit where they wanted to sit. In the lunchrooms, the black students sat on one side. The white students sat on the other side. And the ladies' room, it was the same thing. The black students went to the right of the ladies' room; the white students went to the left of the ladies' room. So really, it was separate. I mean, we attended the same school, but we never really did anything together.

Another woman who was bused to South Boston in 1974 recalled, "It was hard to learn anything. . . . At least twice a week we had an early dismissal; they brought us out the side door any time there was a disturbance. The buses were stoned every other day.

They shouted 'Niggahs! We're gonna burn you!' "

According to many students at the time, the parents were more likely to be opposed to busing than the young people themselves were. As two white students said to reporters in 1974, "The kids get along. It's the parents. We *like* school." Moreover, while many white parents supported busing and sent their kids to predominantly black schools in Roxbury, the media payed attention only to the opposition. As a *Boston Globe* columnist wrote, "To mix Southie and Roxbury . . . was not to ask for war, for the war was inevitable, but it was to ensure that the war would be bloody."

On December 11, 1974, just three months after busing began, a white student was stabbed by a black student during an altercation at South Boston High. The wound was not fatal, but the incident provoked an immediate response from the white community: the security of all the black students at South Boston High was threatened. Fearing retaliatory violence, teachers and administrators separated the students, sending the whites outside to where a huge crowd was beginning to gather, and leaving the black students in the school, protected from the mob outside. As police cars attempted to come up the street, angry whites turned the cars over; they threw stones at mounted police.

The black students inside the school were trapped, and Boston police and black community leaders worked together to devise a plan for evacuating them. A group of black adults volunteered to ride decoy buses that would distract the mob while the students were evacuated. Ellen Jackson, director of a black community center called Freedom House, was one of the volunteers. She described the incident:

So we got on the bus and we tried to joke. We were

lying on the floor. Percy Wilson, who was head of [the Roxbury] Multi-Services [Center] said, "Oh, God, I thought I left these days in Mississippi. I didn't think I would be into this kind of situation again." But we were nervous . . . We came around the front part of the building where the people, the mob—in a sense, crazy mob—was and they could see us. We were slouching so we would look like students. . . And while we were trying to distract them, hopefully distracting them, the two buses with the students would take another route and get down the hill. When we started down that hill, I tell you, they rushed past the police and started rocking those buses. I know they rocked the one I was on. And as we were going down, they started throwing everything they could get in their hands. Not rocks, they looked like boulders . . . And when we got down the hill, it was complete silence on the bus. And I think a lot of us just started crying. Fear and anger and hurt.

"The kids get along," said two white students to reporters in the midst of forced busing in 1974. "It's the parents."

But the decoy worked, and the black students were evacuated safely from South Boston High. For the month following the stabbing, four South Boston schools were closed for a cooling-off period. When they reopened on January 8, 1975, over 400 police officers monitored the arrival and departure of the school buses. Only 876 students out of 3,000 attended on the first day back to school. One black student, showing up for school, was told by black adults to go home, that it was too dangerous. The boy asked, "Is there any teaching going on there today?" and when they said yes, he said, "Well, I'm going."

On January 22, 1975, the United States Commission on Civil Rights urged President Gerald Ford to ensure the enforcement of school desegregation laws, reporting, "We are at a dangerous crossroads in connection with school desegregation. . . . We cannot afford—because of organized resistance in Boston or any other community—to turn back."

Sporadic violence continued in Boston for two years following the initial desegregation of the public schools. In August 1975, black and white inmates at a local prison broke into a full-scale brawl motivated by the racial conflicts in the schools. That same summer, when 500 blacks went to the predominantly white Carson Beach in South Boston to "reassert the rights of all Boston residents to use public facilities," black and white swimmers threw bricks at each other. In January 1976, black and white students at Hyde Park High School fought each other with fists and chairs. And across the city, 500 whites tried to block a major Boston Harbor tunnel during rush hour to protest court-ordered desegregation.

As the city of Boston celebrated the nation's bicentennial anniversary, the mayor led a march against the violence. "Liberty was born in Boston," he said, "and it will flourish here so long as courageous people of high moral principles are willing to speak what is in their hearts."

As in Boston, the struggle to racially balance the nation's schools continued. A more recent incident occurred in October 1989, when the U.S. Court of Appeals told the school board of DeKalb County, Georgia, to dismantle its segregated neighborhood school system and consider busing students, redrawing school zones, or creating magnet schools for greater integration. The school board had blamed the school's racial imbalance on housing patterns, but the court ruled that it was nevertheless the school board's responsibility to take measures against segregation.

In an ironic shift, some city school boards have considered establishing segregated schools to help needy students. In 1991, both the Detroit and Milwaukee boards of education approved all-male academies for black students within the city's public school system, hoping to reverse a negative trend: black males have the highest drop-out rates, and in Milwaukee, where black males represented 27 percent of the public school population, they were receiving 50 percent of all suspensions. Opponents charged that the move toward all-male black academies was a return to segregation, but proponents believed that the schools would give extra support to an at-risk population.

Whatever the strategies and results of the nation's struggle to racially balance its schools, guaranteeing all children equal educational opportunities in the public schools remains the first step toward building promising futures for all of America's children.

3

"TO GET BEYOND RACISM"

In the 1970s, just as African Americans began to reap the legal gains from the hard-fought civil rights battles of the 1950s and 1960s, they began to lose economically. In the years following the Gary Convention, black Americans had better chances at getting unskilled jobs because of legal inroads that were being made, but those jobs were fast disappearing: manufacturers were abandoning northern cities for the South and the suburbs; automation was eliminating many positions; and a rising federal minimum wage was making employers reluctant to hire unskilled workers. Moreover, inflation was stagnating the economy. The Arab oil embargo of 1973 caused an energy crisis that led to layoffs at manufacturing plants and to a recession in the auto industry. Black workers consequently found it harder to get jobs in the 1970s than at any time since the Great Depression. They needed job training and education if they were going to compete with other workers for limited opportunities.

Applicants wait for unemployment benefits in Detroit. Once a mecca for automotive workers, Detroit's manufacturing industry collapsed after the 1960s, and African Americans in the city were hard hit.

Not only did black workers face this difficulty, but they also continued to be obstructed by racism. In 1973 alone, the U.S. Department of Justice filed 15 civil rights suits to desegregate 24 bars, liquor stores, and pool halls in seven southern states. The owners/operators of these establishments were charged with violating the public accommodations section of the 1964 Civil Rights Act. Thus, nearly 10 years after the passage of that landmark civil rights legislation, African Americans were still living with segregation, which was only the most visible example of the racism that continued to pervade American society.

To combat the disadvantages and racism faced by African Americans, the Kennedy and Johnson administrations had developed a public policy called affirmative action. Mandating that job applicants and employees be treated "without regard to their race, creed, color, or national origin," affirmative action was originally designed to ensure that minorities had an equal opportunity to attain positions based on their merit; but soon it had become a measure to compensate historically underprivileged groups for previous discriminatory practices and to integrate them into all levels of the nation's economy. President Lyndon Johnson explained the problem facing many black Americans in a graduation speech at Howard University in 1965:

> You do not take a person who, for years, has been hobbled by chains and liberate him, bring him up to the starting line of a race and then say, "You are free to compete with the others," and still justly believe that you have been completely fair. Thus it is not enough just to open the gates of opportunity. All our citizens must have the ability to walk through those gates. This is the next and most profound stage of the battle for civil rights. We seek not just freedom but opportunity. We seek not just legal equity but human ability, not just equality as a right and a theory

but equality as a fact and equality as a result.

President Lyndon B. Johnson making the 1965 commencement address at Howard University. "It is not enough just to open the gates of opportunity," he told the audience at the all-black college. "All our citizens must have the ability to walk through those gates."

Eleanor Holmes Norton, who was named head of the Equal Employment Opportunity Commission in 1977, said that "the affirmative action tool was invented only after years of appalling evidence showed that discrimination immobilized some groups in the workplace." But, she maintained, "it ought to be temporary." Once the numbers of minorities in jobs and universities reflected those of the society as a whole, she said, affirmative action could be discontinued.

Many early affirmative action campaigns were highly successful. With the election of its first African-American mayor in 1973, the city of Atlanta, for example, initiated one of the most aggressive campaigns in the nation. Atlanta's population was over 50 percent African American, and it was a mecca for middle-class blacks with college degrees—but 29 percent of the city's black residents lived below the poverty line. Mayor Maynard Jackson encountered intense opposition from Atlanta's white power structure when he implemented an affirmative action plan that involved 20-percent minority participation in the construction of Atlanta's new airport.

Emma Darnell, an African-American woman, was responsible for making sure that minority contractors and workers were granted opportunities with the construction project. "We were for all practical purposes engaged in a revolution," Darnell said. "We knew that's what it was. It was still the civil rights revolution. Those persons during the '60s laid down their lives and died to put us in these positions of power. We did not consider those positions of power to be ends in and of themselves."

The "revolution" worked, however, in Atlanta. According to George Berry, assistant manager of the airport project under Mayor Jackson,

> We were able to convince the architects, engineers, and contractors to modify their position and seek out minority joint-venture partners, to seek out qualified minority-owned contracting firms, and to reach [the mayor's] goal of twenty percent minority and another five percent small businesses. Roughly a hundred and twenty-five million dollars was done by minorities. In those days, that amount of money was historic!

Tom Cordy, an Atlanta businessman who got his first big break on the Atlanta airport project, maintained that affirmative action was an essential key to unlocking opportunities for black Americans, particularly for minority entrepreneurs who wanted to enter the mainstream business community. "We've had an emergence of several firms that have had an opportunity to have access to opportunity. . . . They've been able to grow and develop, and they've become a part of the system."

Efforts to encourage minority employment have

been successful elsewhere in the nation as well. In 1974, the Equal Employment Opportunity Commission and the U.S. departments of labor and justice negotiated with nine major U.S. steel companies until they agreed to a five-year plan to end job discrimination against minorities. The companies also agreed to grant backpay of more than $30 million to people who were the victims of such bias. And Jesse Jackson, founder of Operation PUSH, was able in 1981 to convince executives of corporations patronized by black Americans, such as Coca-Cola, to spend $14 million with minority vendors and to increase black management on staff from 5 to 12.5 percent. Jackson reached similar agreements with other large corporations, such as Kentucky Fried Chicken, Anheuser-Busch, 7-Up, and Burger King.

Despite these advances assisted by affirmative action, the policy has been widely disputed since its creation. It has also changed over time, from an executive order forbidding racial discrimination to a series of policies designed to bring specific numbers of minorities into the workplace. This practice of setting quotas has been one of the most debated aspects of affirmative action. "Most Americans would support what was called affirmative action back in the '60s, programs where efforts were made by companies and colleges to go outside the mainstream in their recruiting," said economist Walter Williams. "But that's an entirely different thing from having hard and fast racial quotas—hiring people according to their numbers in society."

Thomas Sowell, an African-American scholar and an outspoken critic of affirmative action, argues that proportional representation in affirmative action programs is absurd because people do not choose professions in proportion to their numbers but as a result of interest, aptitude, and background. Sowell has argued, "One-quarter of the pro-hockey players in the

U.S. are from Minnesota; more than one-quarter of all American Nobel Prize winners are Jewish; more than one-half of all pro-basketball players are black." If these groups' participation in these professions were limited according to their numbers in society, he contends, mediocrity would be the result.

One dispute about quotas reached the courts in Berkeley, California, in 1975. A 1972 Affirmative Action Act demanded that the city hire minorities for its fire department in proportion to their numbers in the city. But in 1975 this practice was overruled after whites complained that minorities who scored lower on examinations were being hired and promoted on the basis of race. In what seemed a twisting of the objectives of affirmative action, a judge ruled that ignoring exams and hiring on the basis of color violated the Civil Rights Act of 1964, which specifically prohibits anyone from receiving "preferential treatment" because of race.

California was also the focus when the debate centered on affirmative action in the nation's public university systems. In 1978, this debate went all the way to the Supreme Court with *Regents of the University of California v. Bakke*. Allan Bakke, a white engineer who decided in his 30s to become a doctor, had been turned down by 12 medical schools, including the University of California at Davis. This took place twice, in 1973 and 1974, when U.C. Davis reserved 16 of the 100 places in its entering class for disadvantaged students: African Americans, Hispanic Americans, and Asian Americans. Blond, blue eyed, of Norwegian descent, and with an excellent academic background, Bakke claimed that he had been the victim of reverse racial discrimination—that he was more qualified than some of those 16 students admitted in his place and that he therefore had been denied admission because of his race.

When the California Supreme Court ruled in

Surrounded by reporters, Allan Bakke attends his first day of classes at the University of California at Davis Medical School in 1978. Bakke won the landmark Supreme Court decision, Regents of the University of California v. Bakke, *in which the Court ruled that U.C. Davis's affirmative action policy was tantamount to reverse discrimination.*

Bakke's favor, the university appealed to the U.S. Supreme Court. The Bakke case was publicized as the most important civil rights case since *Brown v. Board of Education* in 1954 because of its potential impact on the future of affirmative action.

In a courtroom packed with people who had camped all night on the steps of the Supreme Court in order to be guaranteed seating at the appeal, attorney Archibald Cox argued for the University of Cal-

Protesters in Oakland, California, demonstrate against the state's 1977 decision to admit Allan Bakke to the University of California at Davis Medical School. The United States Supreme Court had yet to hear the case.

ifornia. He claimed that race should be a factor in selecting qualified applicants to remedy the effects of discrimination against blacks. "For generations, racial discrimination in the U.S. isolated certain minorities and condemned them to inferior education. There is no racially blind method of selection which will enroll today more than a trickle of minority students in the nation's colleges and universities."

The Supreme Court handed down a divided decision. The court ruled that U.C. Davis's affirmative action policy was the equivalent of reverse discrimination and that Bakke should be admitted to the university. But it also ruled that race could be one of many determining factors in admitting students, because schools have a legitimate interest in promoting student diversity. "To get beyond racism," wrote Justice Harry Blackmun in the *Bakke* case, "we must first take account of race."

Since *Bakke*, the Supreme Court has handed down different decisions on the constitutionality of affirmative action. While Justice William Brennan wrote that federal law "does not prohibit a court from ordering, in appropriate circumstances, affirmative race-conscious relief as a remedy for past discrimination," the court has also ruled against affirmative action employment programs in Florida and Michigan that contained minority set-asides. In 1989, the Supreme Court also decided that workers who are adversely affected by affirmative action programs can file lawsuits claiming discrimination. And the Civil Rights Bill of 1991, which allows monetary compensation to victims of harassment and discrimination based on sex, religion, or disability, also prohibits employers from adjusting test scores on the basis of race, color, religion, sex, or national origin.

Referring to these blows that the Supreme Court dealt to affirmative action and minority set-aside laws, Justice Thurgood Marshall remarked that the decisions "put at risk not only the civil rights of minorities but the civil rights of all citizens. . . . We forget at our peril that civil rights and liberty rights are inexorably intertwined."

The University of California system—the Berkeley campus in particular—again became the focus of the affirmative action debate in 1992, when the Department of Education decided that a special-treatment admissions policy at U.C. Berkeley violated federal law. The U.C. Board of Regents, which oversees the state's university system, approved the ban on affirmative action at the urging of California governor Pete Wilson; he had argued that affirmative action was discriminating against more qualified applicants. Facing a 1998 deadline for eliminating racial preferences in its university system, California admissions departments are struggling with the task of removing racial preferences without destroying student diversity.

Public universities want to reward merit and recruit the most promising students, but they are also responsible for serving the entire public, including minorities who have historically not had access to education. In California, the clash over affirmative action involves black, white, Hispanic-American, and Asian-American students. Some Asian Americans worry that affirmative action has hurt them because on average their scores on entrance exams are the highest of any racial group. Quotas on Asian-American students now are reminiscent of the quotas once used to limit the number of Jews on college campuses.

Disappointingly, studies have shown that students admitted under affirmative action programs have a far higher drop-out rate than those admitted according to traditional criteria. To counteract this trend, both the American Council on Education and the Education Commission of the U.S. have recommended that colleges and universities work with educators at primary and secondary levels to improve the preparation of minority students. Institutions of higher education also need to create a campus culture that values diversity and responds powerfully to racism on campus so minority students will be encouraged to stay enrolled.

The reasons a student admitted under affirmative action may choose ultimately to leave school are suggested by a black freshman at Berkeley who had mixed feelings about affirmative action. "If that's the only way they can keep all these different cultures here, then I think the system has to stay the same because that's so important in the world we're in now. But sometimes I'm uncomfortable with it. You don't want people to think you got in here because you're black."

Responding to accusations of ignoring minority issues, the Reagan administration claimed a "firm and far-reaching" commitment to civil rights. President Reagan (at the lectern) is joined, second from left, by future Supreme Court Justice Clarence Thomas, whose confirmation hearings raised controversy regarding affirmative action.

Confirmation hearings of Clarence Thomas's nomination to the Supreme Court in 1991 triggered more debate over affirmative action. Thomas, himself the former head of the Equal Employment Opportunity Commission and the beneficiary of an affirmative action program at Yale Law School, was an outspoken critic of affirmative action programs. Consequently, many people felt that Thomas was hypocritical in his stance, although others justified Thomas's decision, charging that the experience of receiving preferential treatment violates human dignity by regarding people as a means to a social end and not as an end in themselves.

Opponents of affirmative action also argue that it has only helped minorities in middle- and upper-income groups, who no longer need preferential treatment. When sociologist William Wilson observed in the 1970s that "talented and educated blacks are experiencing unprecedented job opportunities in the growing government and corporate sectors, opportunities that are at least comparable to those of whites with equivalent qualifications," he also noted that affirmative action programs were most beneficial to those blacks who had the education to qualify for white-collar salaried positions. One of the arguments used by opponents of affirmative action is that it benefits people who have never faced job discrimination and victimizes people who have never practiced discrimination. Some argue that affirmative action programs have created a "glass ceiling" in corporations because managers, unsure of the real qualifications of minorities hired under affirmative action programs, will only promote them so far.

Controversy over affirmative action has been further provoked by the inclusion of other minority groups into its protection. During the 1970s, affirmative action was used to bring more women into the workplace and to assist Vietnam veterans. Hispanic Americans and Asian Americans, two of the fastest-growing immigrant groups, also qualified for protection and preference under affirmative action programs. As more and more groups are included, opposition to the policy grows. And while all immigrant groups have faced prejudice, only African Americans can claim an extended history of institutionalized, legal racism, through the practices of slavery and segregation. As Thurgood Marshall wrote, "the experience of [blacks] in America has been different in kind, not just in degree, from that of other ethnic groups."

Nevertheless, backsliding continued. In the 1980s, the gap between the average incomes of whites and blacks was as wide as it had been more than 20 years earlier, according to a report by the Center for the Study of Social Policy, a Washington research group. In 1960, 74 percent of black men over 16 were employed, compared to only 55 percent in 1984. In its "State of Black America" report in 1990, the National Urban League (NUL) confessed its belief that to "close the economic gap" between black and white Americans, a $50-billion aid program, similar to the Marshall Plan used to rebuild Europe after World War II, was necessary. The NUL called on the federal government to "complete our unfinished revolution for democracy and civil rights."

Although the debate over its ethical implications goes on, affirmative action has increased educational and employment opportunities for minorities and for women of all races. Affirmative action has demanded the full participation of all groups in American society, making the United States today a more inclusive society than at any other time in its history. And this inclusiveness in the workplace and on campus has been matched, since the early 1970s, with the growing presence of African Americans on all levels of the nation's political structures.

"HE CAN
JESSE JACKSON
RUN

4

ROLLING UP THEIR SLEEVES

As Gary mayor Richard Hatcher put it, after the Gary Convention, "People went back home, rolled up their sleeves, and ran for public office in a way that blacks had never thought about running for public office before." For African Americans since the 1970s, taking public office has largely meant attending to the problems faced by the nation's largest cities.

Throughout the 1970s, the nation's cites changed from vibrant social centers with job opportunities and cultural activities to areas inhabited, according to many, only by those who could not afford the suburbs. So-called "white flight" from the cities had left many urban areas with large, poor, black populations, massive bills, and an economic base too weak to pay them. A 1981 survey found that black children in the United States were four times as likely as whites to be born in poverty, twice as likely to drop out of school before 12th grade, five times as likely as white teenagers to be murdered, and three times as likely to be unemployed. The high unemployment rate was

Jesse Jackson and his Rainbow Coalition proved enormously powerful in catching the nation's attention and pulled together voters of all races.

related to the increase in the number of black families headed by single women, many of whom were unmarried teenagers forced to rely on welfare to support their children.

As the situation for poor blacks worsened, the black middle class in America expanded. By the 1970s, a schism had opened between the black poor and the black middle and upper classes. The latter were growing larger and dispersing geographically, moving to suburban areas, while the black "underclass" expanded too and became isolated in the inner cities. Class, more than race, now determined black opportunities.

Public-opinion surveys began to show strong differences of opinion among blacks, making black solidarity on basic issues even more difficult to achieve than it had been at the Gary Convention. Faced with these obstacles to overcome, African Americans continued to run for office and to seek political empowerment in the hope of finding solutions to the many problems confronting them.

After Gary, there had been a surge of success among black candidates for mayoral offices. In 1973, Maynard Jackson was the first black man elected mayor of Atlanta, and Tom Bradley won the mayor's office in Los Angeles. In 1976, Unita Blackwell, a founding member of the Mississippi Freedom Democratic Party, became the first black female mayor in the history of Mississippi; this occurred in Mayersville, where for much of her life she had been denied the right to vote.

Developing a base of black registered voters was crucial to the continued success of black political candidates. In 1982, African Americans in Chicago, led by Jesse Jackson and Operation PUSH and by other grass-roots organizations, instituted a massive voter-registration drive to increase the black voter base. Black Chicagoans wanted to elect a black

Hattie Lee Brown, a Miami Beach woman with nine children, was evicted from her one-bedroom apartment in 1972. Her situation painfully illustrates the persistent problems faced by poor, female-headed black families—problems that would challenge all those entering politics after the Gary Convention.

mayor, and they had their candidate, Harold Washington; they had the voting-age population to put him in office; but first they had to motivate people to register and to care about voting.

When a registration activist approached Ed Gardner, chairman of the board of Soft Sheen Products, a hair-care product company he started in 1964 in his basement, Gardner agreed to donate a quarter of a million dollars—as well as his corporation's marketing and advertising departments—to help create a campaign that would encourage blacks in Chicago to register to vote. The slogan "Come alive October 5" appeared on television ads, radio spots, banners, and T-shirts around the city. Years later, Gardner recalled how pervasive that campaign was in Chicago—

New York Congresswoman Shirley Chisholm campaigning in Florida for the 1972 presidential election. Although her effort to secure the Democratic nomination fell short, she was the first woman and the first African American to run for the country's highest office.

reaching almost every level of society:

> I remember one time I walked into a gas station . . . I paid for my gas . . . and the fellow said—this fellow could hardly speak his name; he wasn't the sharpest fellow in the world—last thing he said, "Have you registered to vote?" Now you know, to me, when I reached the person who you think is insignificant in this city and voting is important to him, we were extremely successful.

By October 5, 1982, Chicago had over 100,000 new black voters. Harold Washington, then a representative of Illinois in Congress, won the Democratic nomination for mayor of Chicago, defeating incumbent mayor Jane Byrne and contender Richard Daley, son of the late Mayor Daley. On election day, black voters turned out in unprecedented numbers to elect Washington, making him the first African-

American mayor of the city of Chicago.

Black Chicagoans felt great pride in having one of their own elected to head the city. One elderly man, who was determined to get to the polls on election day, had struggled along the sidewalk with his walker. Stopping to rest, he refused those who offered him a ride to the polls. "No," he said. "I want to go on my own and vote for that boy."

Since the early 1970s, African Americans have made progress in the realm of national and state politics as well. Blacks have become members of Congress in high numbers, campaigned for the presidency, been appointed to presidential cabinets, and been elected to state governorships.

African Americans had gained serious ground in Congress through the Congressional Black Caucus (CBC), a group dedicated to the interests of black America, which was formed in 1971 when the nine black representatives then in Congress decided to come together and share the responsibility of working on behalf of all black people. These representatives felt they had a commitment not just to their individual constituencies but to the black nation as a whole. The official motto of the CBC is "Black people have no permanent friends, no permanent enemies, just permanent interests."

African Americans had long debated running for high office, and the first person to break the race barrier in presidential primaries was a black woman. In 1972, Representative Shirley Chisholm of New York, the first black woman to serve in Congress, announced that she would seek the Democratic presidential nomination and that her candidacy "would help repudiate the notion that the American people would not vote for a qualified black or female candidate." Although black male leadership (including the CBC) dismissed her candidacy, Chisholm remained undaunted. She competed in 10 primaries, won 35 delegates, and received 151 of 2,000 votes cast at the 1972 Democratic convention, which nominated George McGovern. Although Chisholm's bid for the presidency fell short, it nevertheless was a symbolic landmark. More tangible steps soon followed in the realm of presidential politics.

Perhaps one of the most dramatic changes occurred during the 1976 presidential election, when Jimmy Carter, who received 90 percent of the black vote, defeated President Gerald Ford. The Carter Administration appointed many African Americans to policy-making positions, including Eleanor Holmes Norton, the first African-American woman (and first woman) as chair of the Equal Employment Opportunity Commission; and Patricia Roberts Harris as secretary of Housing and Urban Development, the first black woman to serve in a presidential cabinet.

The next African American to seek the presidential nomination was Jesse Jackson. A longtime activist and former coworker of Martin Luther King, Jr., Jackson had founded Operation PUSH in 1971 to help organize economic and educational programs for the poor. Jackson became known as black America's "ambassador" when he visited the Middle East in 1979 to discuss long-term peace settlements between Israel and Palestine with Syrian president Hafez Al-Hassad and Palestine Liberation Organization leader Yasser Arafat. Though Jackson's visit angered many pro-Israeli Americans, it forged a friendship with Syria that Jackson was able to use in 1983, when he convinced the Middle Eastern country to return Lieutenant Robert Goodman, a black air force officer who had been taken prisoner after his plane was shot down over Syria.

Jackson's political support came from African Americans and the National Rainbow Coalition, Inc., which he organized in 1984. Announcing his candidacy in 1983, Jackson garnered 300 delegates for the 1984 Democratic National Convention, and blacks voted in record numbers around the country in support of Jackson's bid. At the 1984 Democratic Convention, held in San Francisco, Unita Blackwell, the first black female mayor in Mississippi, was invited to speak. She later recalled,

> I tried not to get too emotional about it [speaking], but there was a feeling that it was worth all of it that we had been through. I remember a woman told me one time when I was running for justice of peace, 'The reason why I won't vote for you is because they going to kill you.' The whites had told her that they were going to kill me, and she thought she was saving my life. And when I stood on that podium twenty years later, I was standing there for this woman, to understand that she had a right to register to vote for whomever she wanted to, and that we as a people were going to live. . . .

Although Jackson won 17 percent of the vote at the 1984 convention, he was allotted only 10 percent of the delegates. Unhappy with the Democratic National Committee's standard methods for distributing delegates, he supported only with reluctance the Democratic presidential and vice-presidential nominees Walter Mondale and Geraldine Ferraro.

Jackson's campaign had in fact been hurt by an off-the-record remark reported in the *Washington Post*, in which Jackson had referred to New York City as "Hymie Town," a reference that many considered a racial slur against Jewish Americans. This remark, along with Jackson's association with Nation of Islam minister Louis Farrakhan, caused Jackson to lose support from Jewish Americans as well as other African Americans. Many Democrats believed that the Jackson campaign was futile and divisive at a time when unity was needed to defeat the Republican incumbent, Ronald Reagan. Indeed, Reagan was reelected in 1984 by the largest margin in recent history. He received 20 percent of the black vote.

By the time of the 1988 presidential campaign, black representation in state legislatures, courts, and school boards was increasing, especially in the South. Jackson decided to campaign again with a new strategy. Learning from his 1984 bid, he ran a campaign in 1988 in which he avoided the appearance of being strictly a "black agenda" candidate while stressing the need for solidarity among black voters. He used his populist theme in the black ghettoes, with the white working class, among southern and midwestern farmers, and in the nation's rural towns.

At the 1988 Democratic National Convention, Jackson placed second in the Democratic presidential primary, losing to then-governor of Massachusetts, Michael Dukakis. Many blacks believed Dukakis would choose Jackson for the vice president's slot, and when Jackson was passed over for the position, many were disappointed. Critics accused Jackson of moving the Democratic party too far to the left, thus resulting in its defeat to the Republican nominee, George Bush, in the 1988 election. There were, however, at least two benefits to the black community from Jackson's campaign: within a year, Douglas Wilder was elected governor of Virginia, and David Dinkins was elected mayor of New York, coups many attributed in part to Jackson's efforts to reduce white antipathy to electing blacks to high office.

When Douglas Wilder—the first African American to be governor of a state—took the oath of office as governor of Virginia in 1990, he declared,

> I am a son of Virginia. . . . We mark today not only a victory of party or the accomplishments of an individual but the triumph of an idea, an idea as old as America, as old as the God who looks out for us all. It is the idea expressed so eloquently from this great commonwealth by those who

Surrounded by his three children, L. Douglas Wilder is sworn in as governor of Virginia in 1990. The first African American to win a state gubernatorial office, Wilder seemed to many to skirt the issue of race, proclaiming instead, "I am a son of Virginia."

> gave shape to the greatest nation ever known . . . the idea that all men and women are created equal, that they are endowed by their creator with certain inalienable rights: the right to life, liberty, and the pursuit of happiness.

Wilder's emphasis on traditionally shared American values like Christianity and the sanctity of Constitutional rights exemplified the mainstream approach of his campaign. According to the *Wall Street Journal*, "Wilder kept Mr. Jackson at arm's length during a year-long campaign that stressed his mainstream appeal to white voters. Wilder appealed for economic development, not economic empowerment, and talked about racial issues only under duress."

Colin Powell's appointment as chairman of the Joint Chiefs of Staff in 1989 marked two firsts: the general (right) was both the youngest man and the first African American to attain the highest military position in the United States.

Similarly, David Dinkins, who defeated Ed Koch in 1989 to become New York City's first black mayor, had been accused of "selling out" by some in the black community who felt he was not responsive enough to their concerns. Dinkins had strong crossover appeal with white voters precisely because he was not a strictly black agenda candidate.

But what that "black agenda" is has continued to be as difficult an issue as it was during the Gary Convention in 1972. Black conservatives, for example, deplore race-conscious policies, including affirmative action, which they believe lowers black self-esteem and increases racial animosity. Instead, they argue, black leaders should focus on initiative and enterprise for blacks, as well as on the internal problems of the black community—such as unwed mothers, school dropouts, drug abuse, crime, violence, and poverty.

Some of the disparities dividing black political factions even at the most powerful levels came glaringly to light in 1991, when President Bush nominated Clarence Thomas—a black conservative known for his antipathy toward affirmative action—to replace retired Supreme Court Justice Thurgood Marshall. Thomas's confirmation hearings were dominated by the accusation made by one of his former colleagues, Anita Hill, that he had sexually harassed her. During hearings that kept many Americans glued to their television sets, Hill questioned Thomas's propriety in an act that some considered a last-minute attempt to block the confirmation of a conservative judge to the court. Many African American and women's rights leaders came out against Thomas; the NAACP and all but one member of the CBC opposed Thomas's nomination, stating that he did not embody the view of the majority of black Americans—again raising the question of whether there was only one valid interpretation of the African-American experience.

Polls have indicated sharp differences in opinion between upper-, middle-, and lower-income African Americans, demonstrating that there cannot be one interpretation of the black experience in America. Professor Stephen Carter has written about the problematic issue of "the black experience" in terms that recall the Gary Convention's organizing slogan, "Unity Without Uniformity":

> I frequently receive letters from a variety of organizations that begin with something like 'Dear minority colleague' and go on to treat me as though I already agree with the organization's goals and strategies. . . . Surely the minimum obligation of black people to one another is to accord the

respect that comes from acknowledging that we fairly sparkle with diversity of outlook. . . . We need solidarity, we need unity, not in the sense of group think, but of group love.

Indeed the fundamental division among those who attended the Gary Convention in 1972 has remained in place: it is a polarity between those who seek political strength within the existing power structure and those who insist on remaining outside it.

Among those who have struggled within the power structure, there have been—as evidenced by the number of African Americans attaining positions as mayors, governors, and Congressional representatives—great successes. The CBC, for example, has grown; today it includes Carol Moseley-Braun (a Democrat from Illinois), who in 1992 became the first African-American female senator, and Gary Franks (a Republican from Connecticut), the first Republican member of the predominantly Democratic CBC. Franks's 1990 election in a district that is not predominantly black demonstrates that whites will vote for black candidates who share their political views.

Furthermore, in 1992, at both the Republican and Democratic conventions, African Americans played many influential roles; for the first time, blacks dominated administrative positions. Ron Brown, who was the top strategist for Jesse Jackson's 1988 campaign, was chairperson of the Democratic National Committee and led the 1992 Democratic National Convention in New York. That year, Bill Clinton was elected, receiving 82 percent of the black vote. For his inauguration in January 1993, Clinton asked poet Maya Angelou if she would read a poem. Angelou, the first black poet to read at a presidential inauguration, prepared "On the Pulse of

U.S. senate candidate Carol Moseley Braun joins hands with presidential candidate Bill Clinton and his running mate, Al Gore, during the 1992 election campaign. Her subsequent victory made her the first African-American female senator in history.

Morning," and recited it on national television on the president's inaugural day.

Under the Clinton Administration, five African Americans were appointed to the cabinet: Hazel O'Leary as secretary of energy, Lee Brown as director of the Office of National Drug Control Policy, Jesse Brown as secretary of veteran affairs, and Mike Espy as secretary of agriculture. Ron Brown, the first African American to chair a national political party, was also the first black to be appointed secretary of commerce, a position he held until his death in 1996, when an air force plane, carrying him and a delegation of American business leaders on a mission to develop U.S. trade, crashed outside Croatia. The first cabinet member to die in the line of duty in 150 years, Ron Brown was deeply mourned: "Without him," President Clinton told the nation, "I wouldn't be here," a reference to Brown's leadership role as chair of the 1992 Democratic Committee.

Colin Powell is another African American to gain new ground for blacks within existing political structures. In 1989, the four-star general was named chairman of the Joint Chiefs of Staff, the highest military position in the country. At 52, Powell was the youngest man, and the first African American, to hold this position. Born in Harlem to West Indian immigrants, he rose through the ranks of the military, where he orchestrated the campaign against Iraq during the Persian Gulf War of 1991. At that time, 104,400 of the 400,000 U.S. troops in the Gulf were African American. Powell, who considers the U.S. military "the greatest equal opportunity employer around," was regarded by many as a leading candidate to win the presidential nomination in 1996, but he declined to run for office.

While some African Americans have looked to the existing American political and economic system for empowerment, others have continued to find alternative—nationalistic—means for advancement. Nationalist groups like the Black Panther Party (BPP), which had been organized in 1966 and opposed established channels of authority in the United States, acted on behalf of black empowerment into the 1970s although its leadership had been disbanded. In 1980 and 1984, for example, Angela Davis, who had become involved with the Black Panthers in 1970, ran for vice-president on the Communist party ticket. Under the leadership of Elaine Brown, who was elected chairperson of the BPP in 1974, the BPP increased voter registration, which resulted in the election of the first black mayor of Oakland, California, in 1977.

Probably the most powerful black nationalist organization to gain in popularity since the 1970s has been the Nation of Islam. The members of the Nation of Islam—known as Black Muslims—advocate racial separatism and racial pride and have generally been held at arm's length by mainstream black leaders. By the time of the funeral of Nation of Islam leader Elijah Muhammad in 1975, the Black Muslims had grown influential enough that eulogies were given by such black leaders as Jesse Jackson, Georgia congressman Julian Bond, and several prominent Christian ministers. Led by Louis Farrakhan after the death of Elijah Muhammad, the Nation of Islam experienced a revival in the 1980s and 1990s.

This trend toward nationalism, culminating in the Million Man March on Washington, D.C., in 1995, has become increasingly apparent in American society, as new strains of black culture and expression are embraced by the public at large.

March 30, 1981 / $1.25
Newsweek
Black Magic
Novelist Toni Morrison

5

FROM *ROOTS* TO RAP

The 1970s saw the flowering of the black consciousness movement, a new age of Afrocentricity that affected the media and cultural and educational institutions, giving black culture increased visibility and influence. Together with affirmative action policies, the movement changed the ethnic and racial makeup of the nation's schools, which began to recruit minority faculty members and to alter their curricula, developing courses and programs in African-American studies. The black consciousness movement also influenced writers, artists, and musicians, finding expression in the full range of American culture and media.

Beginning with ground-breaking programs in the 1970s, television began to portray more African Americans in shows that received some of the highest prime-time ratings. *Sanford and Son*, which featured comedian Redd Foxx as an ornery junk dealer from Watts, a section of Los Angeles, premiered in 1972. It ran for five years, and its popularity earned Foxx one of the highest salaries of any television star

Her prodigious storytelling, richly infused with African-American history, has won novelist Toni Morrison popular success, critical acclaim—and the 1993 Nobel Prize in literature.

at that time, close to $25,000 per episode. Another program featuring working-class blacks was *Good Times* (1974–79). Set in Chicago's Cabrini-Green housing project, the show featured Esther Rolle as mother and maid Florence Evans. The Evanses' oldest son, J.J., played by comedian Jimmie Walker, thrilled audiences with his crazy get-rich schemes and his humor—with "Dy-no-mite!" becoming his much-mimicked trademark.

Moving beyond portrayal of working-class black life was *The Jeffersons*, which premiered in 1975 and ran for 11 seasons, becoming television history's longest-running black program. A spin-off from *All in the Family*, *The Jeffersons* featured Isabel Sanford (Louise) and Sherman Hemsley (George) as the former neighbors of white bigot Archie Bunker, who were "movin' on up" due to the success of George's dry-cleaning business. *The Jeffersons* was the first television show to portray a wealthy black family and to introduce a biracial couple to American audiences. *The Cosby Show*, which ran from 1985 to 1992, became the most watched situation comedy in the history of television. It portrayed the Huxtables, an upper middle-class black family that defied stereotypes and was comfortable with its success.

Since the early 1980s, network situation comedies featuring black characters of all economic levels have proliferated. Programs catering to an African-American audience became available through Black Entertainment Television (BET), the brainchild of Robert L. Johnson, which began in 1980 as a cable company broadcasting from Washington, D.C. In 1986, Oprah Winfrey became the first black woman to host a nationally syndicated talk show, and one of America's most recognized figures. And by the 1990s, Ed Bradley, Bryant Gumbel, and Carole Simpson had become familiar, highly respected figures in network news programming.

LeVar Burton as the young Kunta Kinte in Roots, *the 1977 television miniseries based on Alex Haley's best-selling book. The series was showered with Emmy Awards and helped foster a surge of interest in African-American studies.*

One of the most notable sensations in the black consciousness movement of the mid-1970s took the form of both a book and a television program: Alex Haley's *Roots*, published in 1976, was an autobiographical attempt to trace his African-American ancestry. The book sold 1.6 million copies in its first six months of publication, was translated into 22 languages, and won Haley a special Pulitzer Prize. The book was also adapted into a 12-hour television miniseries that aired in January 1977 and was watched by 130 million Americans. The book and

Oprah Winfrey earned an Oscar nomination for her portrayal of the imposing Sofia in The Color Purple *in 1985. She followed up this accomplishment by becoming the first black woman to host a nationally syndicated talk show in 1986.*

program had a profound effect upon many young Americans and encouraged a wave of interest in black genealogy and in literature about African-American history. Other black male writers who have gained prominence in the literary world include Charles Fuller, James McPherson, and Ishmael Reed.

A renaissance of black women writers occurred in the 1980s, with popular authors like Toni Morrison, Alice Walker, Jamaica Kincaid, Maya Angelou, Rita Dove, and Terry McMillan dominating the publishing scene. Toni Morrison began as a scholar and editor, responsible for publishing various books by black writers. She published her first novel in 1969, but it was not until the late 1970s that she gained renown with *Song of Solomon*. Morrison's Pulitzer Prize–winning *Beloved*, published in 1987 and inspired by the true story of a runaway slave, expresses the painful legacy of slavery and speaks of the need to bear witness for the enslaved. It was Morrison's fifth novel, part of a body of work that won the author a Nobel Prize for literature in 1993—the first awarded to an African-American woman.

In 1982 Alice Walker published *The Color Purple*, about a young woman's painful experiences growing up in rural Georgia. The book won a Pulitzer Prize and became a best-seller; it was further popularized by Steven Spielberg's 1985 film adaptation, which featured stars Whoopi Goldberg and Oprah Winfrey. Although the film was attacked by some for not accurately representing "the black experience," it was vehemently defended by many, including Goldberg, as being no more obliged to represent "the black experience" than a film featuring white characters would be expected to represent "the white experience."

Filmmaker Spike Lee emerged in the 1980s with more new media representations of black Americans. His 1989 film, *Do the Right Thing*, set on a hot summer day in a Brooklyn neighborhood, shows the events leading up to an outbreak of racial violence. The movie features rap group Public Enemy's song "Fight the Power" from *It Takes a Nation of Millions to Hold Us Back*. Movie critic Roger Ebert called *Do the Right Thing* "the most honest, complex and unblinking film [he had] ever seen about the subject of racism." Spike Lee also directed *Malcolm X*, a feature film about the slain Black Muslim leader. When Lee ran over budget while making the film, a number of wealthy African Americans—including Bill Cosby, Oprah Winfrey, Janet Jackson, the artist formerly known as Prince, "Magic" Johnson, Michael Jordan, and philanthropist Peggy Cooper Cafritz—came together in an act of economic solidarity to help Lee complete the film.

An act of solidarity on a larger scale took place within the music industry in 1985, when singer Michael Jackson collaborated with Lionel Richie and producer Quincy Jones to create "We Are the World," a number-one single that was sung by the largest gathering of musical celebrities in history to benefit African famine-relief efforts. With the 1982 release of his *Thriller* album, Michael Jackson, formerly of the Jackson 5, sold over 40 million copies. In 1988, *Forbes* reported that Michael Jackson, then 30 years old, was the world's highest-paid entertainer, earning $60 million that year.

Although Jackson may be the most financially successful black singer to emerge since the 1970s, hundreds have risen to stardom with songs and albums that show the diversity of black music. Singer and composer Stevie Wonder has steadily fused musical experimentation with political and social content in a career that has so far won him more than 15 Grammy Awards and an Academy Award. Donna Summer became America's disco queen with "Love to Love You Baby" in 1975, which hit number two on the *Billboard* charts. Tina Turner's *Private Dancer* album, released in 1984, eventually went platinum and marked Turner's success since leaving her husband and collaborator, Ike Turner, and embarking on her own. On the jazz scene, pianist and composer Errol Garner was the best-selling jazz pianist in the world in 1977, most well known for his work "Misty." In 1984, trumpeter Wynton Marsalis became the first musician to win Grammy Awards for jazz and classical recordings simultaneously. That same year, the composer, producer, and artist then known as Prince released the soundtrack to his film *Purple Rain*, winning an Oscar and several Grammys. Popular and

The 1985 single "We Are the World" was the brainchild of Michael Jackson, Lionel Richie, and Quincy Jones. Recorded by the largest group of music stars ever assembled, the song benefitted famine-relief efforts in Africa.

financial successes have continued in the 1990s: four young crooners called Boyz II Men, for example, broke Elvis Presley's 1956 record in 1992 when their single "End of the Road" stayed at number one on the pop charts for 13 weeks.

Alongside these successes in commercial pop music has been the steady development of alternative voices in African-American music culture. The early 1970s saw the rise not just of disco but also of funk, a much grittier sound whose roots may be found in the music of James Brown and Sly and the Family Stone, and which is epitomized by the music of Parliament-Funkadelic. But perhaps the most influential sound to emerge since the mid-1970s has been rap.

In 1980, the Sugar Hill Gang's "Rapper's Delight" was released and gained wide airplay, marking the beginning of a new musical genre that would grow into a national phenomenon over the next decade.

Chuck D, Terminator X, and Flavor Flav of Public Enemy aggressively address problems of urban life in songs like "Fight the Power" and "911's a Joke."

Rap had begun in the 1970s when DJs, using two turntables and a sound mixer, started sampling—playing instrumental breaks from popular records and switching from one to another to create a unique, never-ending dance mix. Using a microphone, a master of ceremonies (MC) could call to the crowd and create original rhymes. Clive Campbell (a.k.a. Cool Herc), black nationalist DJ Africa Bambaataa from the southeast Bronx, and Josep Saddler (a.k.a. Grandmaster Flash) from central Bronx were among the first rappers, their rhyming talk usually focusing on themselves and their prowess.

Rap culture flourished in cities like New York, L.A., Oakland, and Miami, which had large minority populations hard hit by economic decline and unemployment. By the 1980s, rap was beginning to display strong political and racial awareness, the rhyming essays speaking of life in the ghetto.

In 1985, Russell Simmons, a rap music promoter and manager, founded Def Jam Records and Rush productions, and Def Jam became home to rap's biggest artists: Run DMC, Public Enemy, and L.L. Cool J. In 1986, Run DMC's version of Aerosmith's "Walk This Way," the first rap song to achieve mass crossover success, was number one on the *Billboard* charts. When the music channel MTV, which had been accused of racism in its programming choices, debuted "Yo! MTV Raps" in 1988, the program—showcasing rap music and hip-hop culture—quickly became one of the station's most popular programs. Rap has achieved mass appeal in other segments of the population, evidenced by record sales to non-blacks, and has grown into an enormous business, bringing in over $600 million annually. Every major record company has made significant investments in rap music.

Scholar Michael Dyson refers to rappers as "urban griots [chroniclers] dispensing social and cultural critiques." The dominant political ideology of rappers is black nationalism. Public Enemy member Chuck D calls the group's third album, *Fear of a Black Planet*, a statement against "western cultural supremacy." Many rappers, particularly the so-called "gangsta rappers," have been criticized for their racist, misogynist, anti-Semitic, and violent lyrics—many of them echoing the controversial Nation of Islam minister Louis Farrakhan.

While these accusations are valid, gangsta rappers have also been recognized for expressing real-life experiences and exposing the conditions of poor inner-city black Americans. And female rappers like Queen Latifah, MC Lyte, and Salt-n-Pepa, along with co-ed groups like Arrested Development, show that rap is also capable of portraying strong females and positive male-female relations.

But because its lyrics are often violent and sexually explicit, rap has been surrounded by the controversy of censorship. In a move criticized by some as setting a precedent for the censorship of rap, artist Ice-T removed the song "Cop Killer" from his 1992 *Body Count* album. Ice-T's producer, Time Warner, was accused of bowing to pressure from politicians and special-interest groups after initially promising to support Ice-T's First Amendment rights. The group 2

Live Crew also tested First Amendment rights with their *Nasty as They Wanna Be* album, which was the first album to be ruled criminally obscene by a judge. Nevertheless, according to Quincy Jones, one of the most successful black musicians and producers in pop music, "Rap is no fad, and it's not just a new kind of music. It's a whole new subculture that's been invented by the disenfranchised."

Beyond these achievements and self-expressions within the media, perhaps the area in which African Americans have made the greatest accomplishments has been sports. In his book *Hard Road to Glory*, the late tennis star Arthur Ashe wrote about what he believed to be an African-American cultural emphasis on participation in athletics. The racial transformation of professional and other competitive sports from the 1970s to the 1990s is proof of the success and progress of African-American athletes.

Nowhere have black athletes shown more brightly than in professional basketball. Once snubbed from pro ball, African Americans gained an increasing number of roster positions in the National Basketball Association (NBA) in the 1970s. In 1972, Wilt Chamberlain became the first player in the NBA to score 30,000 points in a career. Julius Erving helped revolutionize how the sport was played. Kareem Abdul-Jabbar began playing for the Lakers in 1975 and went on to become the leading scorer in NBA history; he also led the Los Angeles Lakers to five NBA championships. In 1980, Earvin "Magic" Johnson joined the Lakers and became one of the best point guards in the NBA. His 25-year, $25-million contract with the NBA was in 1981 the largest total sum in sports team history.

By the 1980s, the arrival of not only "Magic" Johnson but also Patrick Ewing, Clyde Drexler, Charles Barkley, Michael Jordan, and Hakeem Olajuwon made it apparent that blacks were now the

Clash of the titans: "Magic" Johnson (right) gets around Michael Jordan. In 1981, Johnson signed a 25-year, $25-million contract to play in the NBA. Fifteen years later, Jordan signed for the same amount—for a single NBA season.

dominant force in basketball. Three-quarters of all NBA players were African American—a statistic reflected in the racial makeup of the first Olympic basketball team made of NBA stars; it had 10 black and 2 white players and easily won the gold medal at the 1992 Summer Olympics.

Basketball was one of the first major professional sports to hire black head coaches, but into the 1990s there remained a proportionately small number of black coaches and general managers. In the NBA in 1992, for example, although three-quarters of the players were black, there were only two black coaches. The situation was similar in the National Football League (NFL): in 1992, 60 percent of NFL players were black, but only two head coaches were black. Recently, greater efforts have been made to hire more minorities in sports management positions. Nevertheless, the vast majority of college coaches, trainers, and athletic directors, as in professional sports, are white.

Of all professional sports, boxing has the best record for integration, as many of its fighters, trainers, managers, and promoters are African American. In fact, the sport boasts a long history of famous African-American athletes. Boxer Muhammed Ali edged out baseball great Hank Aaron in 1975 to become the Associated Press's athlete of the year; the award signalled a new acceptance of Ali, who had resumed his career after a three-year ban placed on him for refusing to be drafted during the Vietnam War. Ali won the richest contest in history in 1974, when he knocked out George Foreman in Kinshasa, Zaire, to regain the heavyweight crown in a fight he billed "the rumble in the jungle." "Sugar" Ray Leonard, who won a gold medal for boxing in the 1976 Olympics and the world welterweight title in 1979, was named sportsman of the year in 1981 by *Sports Illustrated* magazine.

In baseball, legend Hank Aaron of the Atlanta Braves broke Babe Ruth's record in 1974 for the most career home runs. Reggie Jackson of the New York Yankees became the first baseball player to hit three home runs during a World Series in 1977. Baseball also had the first black manager, Frank Robinson of the Cleveland Indians, to lead a major league team.

African Americans have excelled in the Olympics as well. In 1984, Evelyn Ashford, Edwin Moses, and Carl Lewis all won gold medals for track and field events. Figure skater Debi Thomas, the world figure skating champion in 1986, was the first African American to win a medal in the Winter Olympics when she received a bronze at the Calgary Games. In the 1988 Summer Games, Florence Griffith Joyner and Jackie Joyner-Kersee took home multiple gold medals in track and field events, and Joyner-Kersee became the first woman to repeat as Olympic heptathlon champion when she won the title for the second time at the 1992 Summer Olympics in Barcelona.

Among the most notable black athletes to grace the sports scene was tennis star Arthur Ashe, who won the men's singles title at Wimbledon in 1975 and became the first black to be ranked as the top tennis player in the world. Smart and gentlemanly, he proved to be one of the most politically active and socially aware athletes of his generation. Ashe, in fact, was the perfect role model—and he emerged in the public eye at a time when people in the sports and entertainment worlds were being looked up to by young Americans more than ever before.

Indeed, the decades following the Gary Convention have marked a time when sports stars and musicians, filmmakers and writers, seem to influence public behavior and attitudes as much as lawmakers and educators do. And it is African Americans who are now at the forefront of this contingent. Back in 1910, when the news was flashed above Times Square that a black boxer, Jack Johnson, had just retained his title as the heavyweight champion of the world, the throng of 40,000 spectators who had gathered on the New York City streets to learn the outcome of the bout left the scene in shock and subdued silence. Now, the circumstances are different. African Americans are on the road to getting their fair share of the glory, and (as a recent promotional campaign put it) everyone wants to "Be Like Mike"—that is, like a black athlete: megastar Michael Jordan.

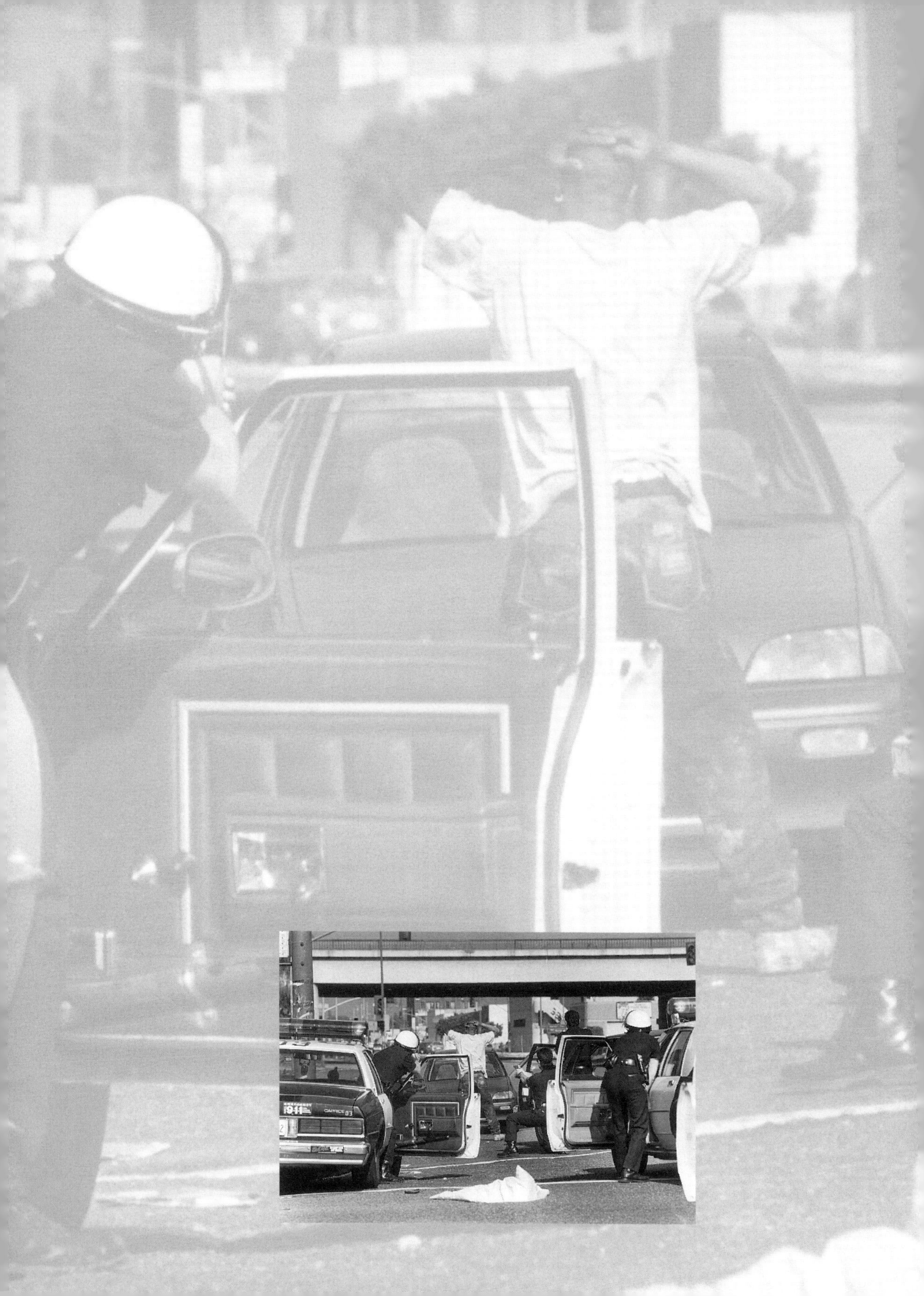
9-1-1
CAPRICE 03

6

CRIMINAL JUSTICE

In 1976, Clarence "Willie" Norris, the last of the Scottsboro Boys—nine black men who had been accused of raping two white women in 1931—was pardoned from the conviction for which he had been sentenced to life in prison. At age 64, Norris, who had escaped from jail in 1946, was declared not guilty. He had spent nearly his entire life either in prison or as a fugitive, convicted for a crime he had not committed.

Although by the mid-1970s African Americans were joining the enforcement and prosecution sides of the U.S. legal system in record numbers, for the majority of black Americans, as for Willie Norris, the criminal justice system had long been synonymous with unfair treatment from white juries, high conviction rates for blacks, and police brutality. In 1972, for example, at Southern University in Baton Rouge, Louisiana, two black students were shot by police during a confrontation on campus. The event mirrored the shootings at Kent State and at all-black

Los Angeles police officers apprehend a suspect—in a scene with chilling similarities to the videotaped arrest of Rodney King—during the days of looting and violence that followed the 1992 King verdict.

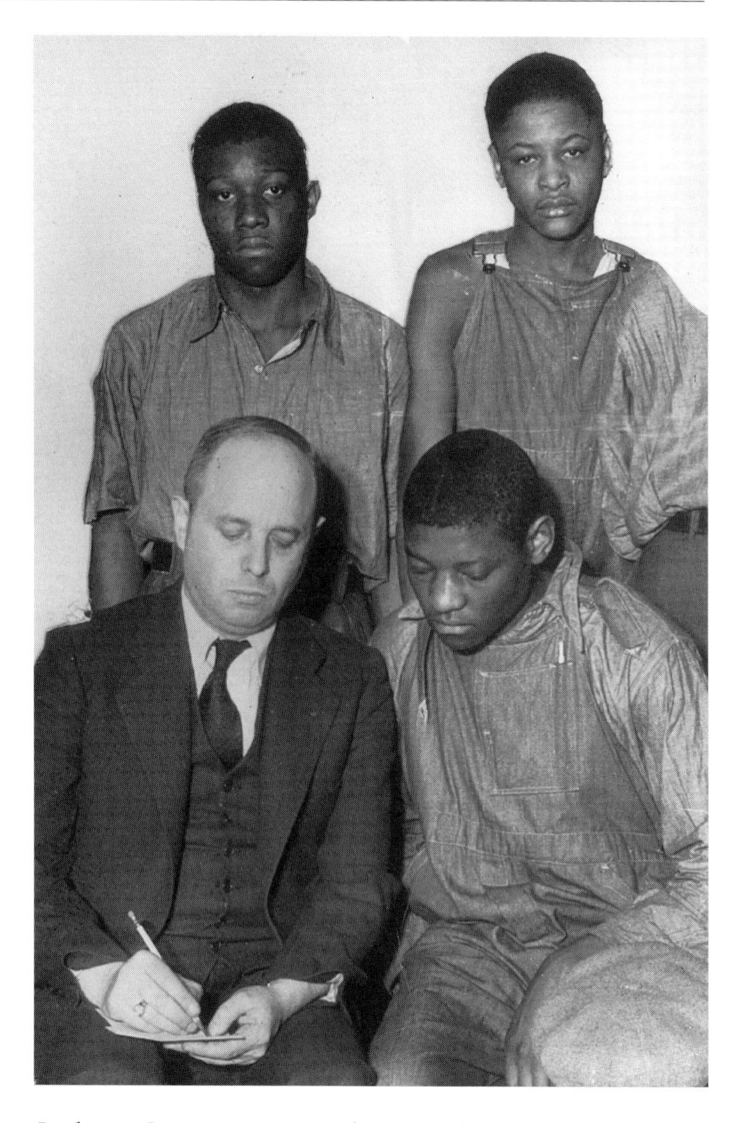

Attorney Samuel Liebowitz with three of the "Scottsboro Boys," the nine black men who were convicted of a 1931 rape of two white women in Alabama. Clarence "Willie" Norris (top left) was found innocent 45 years later.

Jackson State in 1970, where students were killed by police without provocation. A few years later, in 1974, seven people were injured in Atlanta when police officers armed with clubs broke up 250 African-American marchers and arrested 14 people. The marchers had been protesting the killing of a black teenager by police the previous weekend.

"After 350 years of fearing whites," wrote sociologist Charles Silberman in *Criminal Violence, Crimi-*

nal Justice, "black Americans have discovered that fear runs the other way, that whites are intimidated by their very presence. . . . The taboo against expression of anti-white anger is breaking down, and 350 years of festering hatred has come spilling out." This "spilling out" would take place, most visibly in rioting, throughout the 1980s, reaching a peak in Los Angeles in 1992.

In Miami in 1980, a long history of abuses against African Americans and a series of controversial verdicts in cases of police brutality precipitated a racial riot. Violence erupted after a not-guilty verdict was handed down to four Dade County police accused of beating Arthur McDuffie, a black man, to death. McDuffie was a former Marine Corps officer and a successful insurance executive living in Liberty City, a black section of Miami known to the city's predominantly white police officers as a "bad" neighborhood, where they would be sent on patrols as punishment. McDuffie was riding his motorcycle in the evening when, police claimed, he ran a red light and crashed. Police claimed he subsequently resisted arrest, leaving them no choice but to subdue him. But the massive skull fractures and wounds on McDuffie's body were found by the coroner to be consistent with blows of incredible force, not measures taken to subdue a suspect or the results of a motorcycle accident.

Fearing violence, officials decided to hold the trial of the case in Tampa, Florida. There an all-male, all-white jury acquitted the officers of McDuffie's death. Thousands of black Americans protested the verdicts outside the justice building, and fires were started in the streets of Miami. Angry demonstrators began rioting that continued for three days, killing 18 and leaving $100 million worth of damaged property.

The Miami riot came on the heels of a long series of accusations of police brutality against blacks, none of which resulted in significant punishment of the

offenders. Like the rioting in Watts in 1965—which had been prompted by the arrest of a young black man accused of drunk driving, and which led to several summers of intense racial rioting in some of the nation's biggest cities—the Miami riot was a collective expression of anger and frustration.

Several years later, in May 1985, Philadelphia was the site of a disastrous conflict between African

A Florida national guardsman directs traffic away from an uncontrolled fire during three days of riots in Miami in May 1980. The rioting was an outraged response to the acquittal of four police officers believed by many to be responsible for the death of Arthur McDuffie.

Americans and law enforcement officers that many have ascribed to racism. The trouble arose from a conflict between the Philadelphia police and MOVE, a predominantly black group that espoused a number of causes, including protection of the environment and racial justice. But they were also heavily armed and had experienced several clashes with the police over the years. Finally, on May 13, the police moved against them in force, determined to evict MOVE from their row house in a low-income, racially mixed neighborhood. Some members of the group responded with gunfire, much of it coming from a fortified bunker on the roof of the house.

The police believed that if they could knock out the bunker, they would be able to enter the house without major casualties. They decided to blow the bunker apart with a carefully constructed bomb dropped from a helicopter. Unfortunately, the bomb ignited a can of gasoline, and the roof of the house began to burn. Firefighters were on the scene, but half an hour went by before they were sent into action, and by that time, the upper floor of the MOVE house was a mass of flames, and the fire had spread to neighboring houses. Before the firefighters could bring the blaze under control, it had engulfed everything in its path: by the following day, 61 houses had been destroyed and 250 people had lost their homes. Worse still, 11 charred bodies were found inside the rubble of the MOVE house—and 5 of the dead were children.

The episode prompted an outcry that has lasted into the 1990s, with allegations that racism was at the root of the attack on the house: if it had been in a predominantly white neighborhood, critics such as surviving MOVE member Ramona Africa contended, no bomb would ever have been dropped. Nevertheless, the mayor of Philadelphia at the time, W. Wilson Goode, is himself African American: the city's first black mayor and a source of pride for many. Yet this fact has led to suggestions of black-on-black racism and has again underscored the division between separatists and integrationists.

As a result of the tragedy, the police commissioner resigned, but after a two-year inquiry, Goode and his aides were cleared of criminal misconduct. Eleven years after the incident, in June 1996, the city was found guilty in a civil trial.

Racially motivated violence in the burroughs of New York City in the following years further pointed to racist hostility and injustice toward African Americans in the nation's legal structures. Just before Christmas in 1986, a young black man, Michael Griffith, was killed in Howard Beach, a section of Queens, as he tried to escape white attackers. He had entered the mostly white neighborhood when his car had broken down, been pursued, and eventually, in an attempt to flee his pursuers, run onto a parkway and been struck by a car. The three white teenagers convicted in the case were later freed due to the judge's error in instructing the jury in the case.

A few years later, racial violence again disrupted one of the burroughs of New York City. In the summer of 1989, a black teenager, Yusuf Hawkins, and three friends responded to a classified ad for a used car in the predominantly white neighborhood of Bensonhurst, New York. Believing they were visiting a white girl in the neighborhood, several white teenagers attacked Hawkins and his friends, and Hawkins was fatally shot.

Hawkins's death resulted in two days of black demonstrations in Bensonhurst, led by the Reverend Al Sharpton. Over a thousand people attended Hawkins's funeral, where eulogies were given by Mayor Ed Koch, Governor Mario Cuomo, and Black Muslim leader Louis Farrakhan. Filmmaker Spike Lee, who would later create *Do the Right Thing*, a film about racial violence in Bensonhurst, also attended. More than 7,000 protesters shouting "No more!" and "Whose street? Our street!" marched through downtown Brooklyn to the Brooklyn Bridge, where police had set up barricades. When the demonstrators tried to cross the bridge, violence erupted as marchers and police fought hand to hand, rioters threw bottles and rocks, and police beat them back with billy clubs.

Five youths were charged with Hawkins's murder, but ultimately only one was convicted.

The most powerful incident of racial injustice and violence in the United States in three decades, however, was the 1992 Rodney King case and its aftermath in Los Angeles. The economic and social climate in South Central Los Angeles before the incident was not hospitable and in many ways reflected the conditions in inner-city neighborhoods throughout the country. Unemployment among black, Hispanic, and Asian men aged 18 to 35 was nearly 50 percent. Joblessness contributed to growing despair and apathy in the area, which was also afflicted with drug abuse, street crime, and homelessness. Gang violence was common, as members involved in the drug trade had access to weapons that they used in battles with rival gangs and with police. Los Angeles police chief Darryl Gates had angered black and Hispanic community leaders, who complained that the police discriminated against them. In the 1970s, 16 blacks died as a result of police choke holds, and Chief Gates had suggested that blacks had a physical defect that made them susceptible to choking to death. Police officers argued that their work in the inner cities was dangerous, and while they were under pressure to reform their department, they were also being told to assert a stronger police presence on the streets in order to fight crime and drugs.

Although the rioting of 1992 no doubt drew upon this troubled history, it was provoked by a specific incident in 1991: on March 3, police had chased a 25-year-old black construction worker named Rodney King, whose car was speeding at over 100 miles per hour. When police finally stopped him, King was reluctant to get out of the car and resisted arrest while the officers attempted to handcuff him. A two-minute videotape made by a man on a nearby balcony documented how three of the officers beat King with nightsticks while their sergeant looked on. The officers continued to beat King after he was put in restraints and appeared to be incapacitated.

The videotape of the beating was shown on national television, and for many people, it illustrated the urgent need to curb police brutality. Attorneys for the Los Angeles officers, however, used the videotape to convince the jury that Rodney King had continued to act in a dangerous and threatening way during the beating. The officers, who had been charged with assault with a deadly weapon and unnecessary assault and beating, were acquitted by a suburban California jury on April 29, 1992.

The African American community protested the verdicts at once. As the acquitted officers were led away, angry crowds on the steps of the courthouse shouted, "Guilty! Guilty!" and within hours, rage had exploded in the streets of Los Angeles. At first, police tried to break up the riots, but they were overwhelmed by the crowds and forced to retreat. Parts of the city turned into war zones where police had no control: rioters set fires, looted stores and other businesses in South Central Los Angeles, and began to pull passing white motorists from their cars and beat them. There was no one to stop them. Police commander Robert Gil explained how quickly the violence escalated after the King verdict: "With the Watts riots in 1965, it built and built, and on the third day the city went mad," he said. "This was completely different. The city went wild in just an hour and a half."

Most of the destruction and looting occurred in South Central Los Angeles, committed by the people who lived there. There were widespread reports that Hispanic and black rioters were targeting Korean-owned stores: about 60 percent of the stores damaged in the riots belonged to Koreans. Both Hispanics and blacks resented Korean immigrants, who had estab-

His store in flames, a businessman shows the depth of damage inflicted in the black community during the 1992 Los Angeles riots.

lished successful businesses in the middle of predominantly black and Hispanic neighborhoods; the previous year a Korean shop owner had fatally shot a young black girl he suspected of stealing. In the absence of police protection during the riots, many Korean shop owners used weapons to defend their property and fire at would-be looters. Hispanic- and black-owned businesses were also hard hit, with more than 900 destroyed by the rioting. Gangs used the chaos and lack of police patrols to their advantage and organized looting runs in the city. By the second day of the rioting, over 4,000 fires had consumed 25 blocks in South Central Los Angeles.

Rodney King himself appealed for peace: "People," he pleaded, "I just want to say . . . can we all get along? I mean we're all stuck here for a while. Let's try to work it out."

Los Angeles police were criticized for not reacting to the violence more quickly. Police Chief Darryl Gates was out of the city during the initial outbreak of rioting, and the city had not organized a plan of action in case of a disturbance. The police also did not have enough officers to respond effectively to the riots. After the first day of rioting, California governor Pete Wilson sent 750 state patrolmen to Los Angeles and ordered 2,000 National Guardsmen; President Bush called in federal troops. In all, over 10,000 police officers and troops were used to quell the rioters.

By May 2, residents began cleaning up debris from the four days of violence. By then, 52 people had been killed, over 2,000 had been injured, and up to $1 billion of property had been damaged or destroyed. Rioters had destroyed 3,800 buildings and burned, looted, and vandalized another 10,000.

Americans watching coverage of the riots on television were shocked by the violence and destruction exhibited in Los Angeles, and they were forced to look at life in the ghetto. Writer Cornell West addressed the widespread despair, fear, and frustration among African Americans, stating that "the major enemy of Black survival in America . . . is neither oppression nor exploitation, but rather the nihilistic threat—that is, loss of hope and the absence of meaning."

The Los Angeles riots awakened Americans to the problems of the inner cities and helped to focus attention on urban renewal. President Bush declared South Central Los Angeles a disaster area, making it eligible for federal disaster relief money. To organize the massive rebuilding project, Los Angeles mayor Tom Bradley asked former baseball commissioner Peter Ueberroth, head of the Los Angeles Olympic Committee, to lead the Commission to Rebuild Los Angeles. Danny Bakewell, a black entrepreneur and activist, heads the Los Angeles Brotherhood Crusade, which is committed to rebuilding the area's economic base. The two organizations have worked to restore devastated areas. They have encouraged corporations and banks to invest in these areas, and fought to get minority businesses and contractors involved in clean-up related construction and demolition work.

Willie Williams, an African American man, was appointed to replace police chief Darryl Gates. And in 1993, at the civil trial of the officers charged with assaulting King, two of the officers were convicted: one of violating King's right to an arrest "without unreasonable force," and the other of allowing this to happen.

In the wake of the Los Angeles riots, many African Americans lost any remaining faith in the Los Angles Police Department (LAPD). They were convinced that they could not receive justice from the LAPD, and possibly from the criminal justice system as a whole. This antagonism grew in the following years as the LAPD again stood in the national spotlight, during the O. J. Simpson trial.

When former football star Orenthal James Simpson was accused of the 1994 murder of his former wife, Nicole Brown Simpson, and her friend Ron Goldman, his trial became a sensational media spectacle. The case took over nine months, yielded 1,105 pieces of evidence and 45,000 pages of transcripts, and required the jury to be sequestered for 266 days. Although the sheer quantity of evidence against O. J. Simpson was overwhelming, much of that evidence was highly suspect, due to mishandling by police. The detective who had conducted much of the police work in the Simpson case, Mark Fuhrman, proved to be a racist and a perjurer. Faced with a reasonable doubt due to the tampered evidence, the jury stated they had no choice but to acquit Simpson.

O. J. Simpson leaving a Los Angeles police station before being named a suspect in the murder of his former wife and her friend. The subsequent trial became a media extravaganza in which race was a central theme. Simpson's eventual acquittal drew vastly different reactions from blacks and whites.

The verdict divided America. While 83 percent of black Americans agreed with the jury's decision, only 37 percent of whites did.

Black and white reactions to the Simpson verdict show that the differences between black and white Americans are perhaps sharpest in their experiences with the justice system and with the police. One of the most debated aspects of blacks and the justice system centers on the disproportionate number of African Americans in prisons and on death row. While black men make up 6 percent of the country's population, they currently constitute 48 percent of all prison inmates.

Some analysts claim that more blacks than whites are convicted because more blacks commit crimes, in part the result of large African-American populations in inner cities where crime and drug use are escalating. However, other analysts contend, some laws seem to punish blacks more than whites. In mandatory prison sentences for drug possession, for example, federal law distinguishes between crack cocaine, used primarily in the inner city, and powder cocaine, which is more prevalent among wealthy whites. It takes only 5 grams of crack to earn a dealer a 5-year prison sentence, but it takes 500 grams of powder cocaine to earn the same sentence.

The NAACP Legal Defense and Educational Fund maintains that courts discriminate racially, especially when it comes to assigning the death penalty. Former Supreme Court Justice Harry Blackmun, who opposed the death penalty, said that "even under the most sophisticated death penalty statutes, race continues to play a major role in determining who shall live and who shall die."

One of the most alarming trends in the nation's cities is the prediction that violent crime will worsen over the next decade as the black male population between the ages of 14 and 17 grows by 50 percent. The majority of the victims of violent juvenile crime in the cities are also likely to be black. Addressing the root causes of black crime is an essential step to stemming this rising tide. In the words of an African-American woman who works as a juvenile prosecutor, "The police patrol our community, sweeping these young men into jail. But those kids are doing terrible things. If something's wrong with our community, then we've got to fix it, and [if we did] we wouldn't have to be so concerned about the attitudes of white cops."

Eleanor Holmes Norton, former head of the Equal Employment Opportunity Commission and a professor of law at Georgetown University, believes that black Americans need to work alongside the government to rebuild black communities:

> Nobody can reconstruct the black family and bring it to its

historic strength except us. We've got to demand that the programs that should be made available to us in undertaking this work be made available. But also ultimately this is our job and our work. . . . There are going to have to be internal changes in the black community. We've got to halt the precipitous growth of female-headed households. Not only for themselves but because most of those children are being raised in poverty. And thus we cast a pall over the next generation by not giving them a good start in life. We've got to attend to the problems that we don't yet fully understand that are resulting in far fewer black males going to college. Indeed, the whole ghetto pathology that eats up black boys when they're young is something we've got to learn to deal with. There's got to be the reinvigoration and the invention of a galaxy of new programs that originate from the government, taking up models from across the country that have seemed to work. And there's got to be an infusion of young leadership that wants to roll up its sleeves and go to work at the hard problems in the black community that will take more than money.

The African Americans who came to the Million Man March in Washington in 1995, and the countless thousands who supported them from home, signalled that there were many who were prepared to take on these responsibilities.

7

PUTTING THE CHAIN BACK TOGETHER

In October of 1995, African-American men came from all over the country to the nation's capital for the Million Man March. They came to pledge an end to "black-on-black" violence and to renew their commitment to women, children, family, church—and to political activism. The march had been conceived principally by Nation of Islam minister Louis Farrakhan, and, despite controversy surrounding the Nation of Islam's separatist philosophy and accusations that Farrakhan is an anti-Semite, the Nation of Islam minister was able to mobilize a crowd for the march like no other leader. In a time when many traditional black leaders are being called ineffectual, Farrakhan has a reputation for being a doer. "The chain was broken," said a black businessman about the civil rights movement in the 1970s and 1980s. "Farrakhan is helping put the chain back together."

Asked why they were attending the march, few people cited Farrakhan. They came for the cause. "This was an image-building experience, a positive

"Ocean of black manhood": an aerial view of the Million Man March, October 16, 1995. One woman, who attended despite the prohibition against women, described it as the "happiest, most peaceful solemnity [she] will ever witness."

image," said social worker Ray McGill. "We're just bombarded with negative images of black men. It was a counterbalance to all the negative." For 24-year-old Lumumba Bandele, the sheer number of black men who turned out for the march was an inspiration. "On the way down, driving down I-95, you could see who was headed there. Brothers piled up in station wagons. Brothers piled up in their little hatchbacks. Brothers piled up in pick-ups. Everybody is giving the salute, 'All right, all right.' "

African-American men traveling to the Million Man March wanted to defy the negative statistics and images of black men that seem to trap them. Statistics show it is now more likely for a young black man to die from homicide in some areas of the country than it was for a U.S. soldier to be killed on a tour of duty during Vietnam. Black men have a 1 in 24 chance of being murdered, a ratio that is six times higher than that for other Americans. The average life expectancy for an African-American man is 65, which is equal to the average life expectancy of the white male 40 years ago. Black men are 6 percent of the population but make up 48 percent of the prison population. A black man in the U.S. is twice as likely to be unemployed as a white man. Finally, black men are increasingly absent from homes; 60 percent of black women who give birth are single mothers.

The negative images created by these statistics have made black men the most feared population in the country. Indeed, most of downtown Washington was deserted as thousands of office workers stayed home the day of the Million Man March, presumably fearing what events the day might bring. These fears subsided when the day passed without violence, just one of many positive aspects of the Million Man March that day.

At the Mall in Washington, the day's events included praying, singing, a flag-raising ceremony, an

Surrounded by the Fruit of Islam—the Black Muslims' private police force—Nation of Islam leader Louis Farrakhan speaks at the Million Man March, exhorting the crowd to "join organizations that are working to uplift black people."

African dance presentation, and speeches by prominent African Americans in religion, government, business, health, education, and the arts. Marchers met and greeted one another, made new friends, shared stories, sang, and prayed in a show of solidarity that sent a message to the world: despite overwhelming odds, black men are going to make it. Farrakhan told the marchers, "Every one of you must go back home and join some church, synagogue, temple, or mosque, and join organizations that are working to uplift black people."

Debra Dickerson, an attorney from Washington, D.C., initially opposed the march because of Farrakhan's controversial positions and the march's exclusion of women. Dickerson was one of many women who attended the march in defiance of the "men-only" policy, and what she found that day changed her attitude toward the event:

Although the Million Man March was specifically intended for men, poet Maya Angelou was one of several prominent women speakers. Washington mayor Marion Barry stands behind Angelou.

> At the march, my sister and I roamed that ocean of black manhood for eight transfixed hours. It was the happiest, most peaceful solemnity I will ever witness. We saw no alcohol, no empty liquor containers. . . . There was almost none of that male horseplay and loud talk that characterizes typical social situations—the brothers were serious and subdued. . . . We grew hoarse returning the respectful greetings. . . . Paths opened before us; chairs appeared from nowhere; men yanked their sons aside, saying, "Boy, let your auntie by." For an entire, righteous day I was "auntie," I was "sister," I was "daughter." Not "bitch," not "ho," not 'sweet thang.'. . . One rally won't cure black America of its ills, but, when all was said and done, I found myself standing proud, unafraid, and disobedient among one million of my brothers—and finally able to support the march.

The men who had crowded the Mall in Washington returned home, exhausted from all-night bus rides and flights but inspired by a new resolve to improve their lives. They had ideas for voter-registration drives, tutoring programs, food banks, and renewing commitments with their wives. The marchers had made a pledge: "I . . . will strive to improve myself spiritually, morally, mentally, socially, politically, and economically for the benefit of myself, my family, and my people." They left the march with the understanding that they had to take personal responsibility for their lives.

The day after the march, wives, mothers, and daughters in Los Angeles waited in the dark for the men to return. Many of them belonged to "Women Behind the March," a local neighborhood group that had raised over $3,000 to send their men to Washington. Carlotta Pinto waited for her husband, George, who had called her the night of the march. "He called and began telling me how much he loved me and how much he wanted to make what we had work. He hadn't said that to me in years. . . . I haven't heard him this happy in a long time. You wouldn't think one day would do that, but it did."

Critics of the march questioned what one day could really do to improve the position of black men in American, but the personal stories of those who attended the march speak of the power of the gathering to impact the marchers. Former "Crip" gang member Charles Rachal and former "Blood" member Leon Gulette discussed tactics for getting other young people out of gangs like these as they shared a flight home to Los Angeles after the march. Both Rachal and Gulette had quit their gangs after the 1992 riots, and both had gone into housing projects to recruit gang members to come with them to the Million Man March. "You can't imagine what it was like to see opposing gangs hug each other at the march," said Rachal, who spoke briefly at the march, apologizing to families whose sons had died as a result of gang violence.

Ben White, a 28-year-old nurse who came to Washington by bus from Bridgeport, Connecticut, wanted to "experience the feeling of being with [his] brothers." White left Washington with promises "to watch [his] mouth, treat [his] brothers and sisters with respect, get [his] life together and carry the message back to the community."

Atlanta's Southern Christian Leadership Conference (SCLC), which has had trouble attracting new members in recent years, received 100 calls from people seeking volunteer opportunities in the week following the march. Thomas J. Miller, for example, a successful 32-year-old entrepreneur, is letting his wife manage his company so he can volunteer full-time at the SCLC. Miller said the march convinced him that he needed to do more. "My customer base is predominantly black, and it's profitable, but when you see how the community is run-down and degraded, you can't ignore it anymore."

At Frederick Douglass High School in Detroit, 15 young men were sponsored to attend the Million Man March. The students came home with new attitudes toward education, voting, family, women, and responsibility; with plans to raise money for the United Negro College Fund; and with the determination to go to college. "Parents have been calling to thank the school," said the high school's guidance counselor. And elsewhere in the city, where the night before Halloween is traditionally known as "Devil's Night" and is the occasion for vandals to wreak havoc on the city, the Million Man March brought a new spirit of calm. In the weeks following the march, the city's help line received over 15,000 calls from people who volunteered to prevent vandalism and violence as well as to enforce a city curfew.

Although the Million Man March rejuvenated black citizens and encouraged them to organize on behalf of themselves and their communities, there is still a deep need to reconcile America's black and white populations and to curb racism. Recent studies show that African Americans continue to encounter racism, with 60 percent of blacks reporting that they

Former Crips gang member Charles Rachal (center) and former rival Blood member Leon Gulette (right) attended the Million Man March and renewed their commitment to community outreach work. For those who doubted that a day of promises could equal lasting change, Rachal had these words: "This is for real and we are going to see it through."

experience it "at least occasionally." People in higher income brackets experience racism more frequently than those with lower incomes, and those in southern states report less racism than in other regions of the country. Tony Brown, executive producer and host of PBS's *Tony Brown's Journal*, spoke about these statistics:

> It doesn't surprise me that southern blacks find less racism. If blacks had marched in Bensonhurst and Howard Beach thirty years ago instead of Selma, then the whites in Bensonhurst and Howard Beach would be as sensitive today to racism as whites in Selma are. . . . Through our achievements, our unity, through faith in ourselves, sharing our resources, we must make gains that will destroy the environmental supports of racism.

One instance of this type of effort working took place just a few years before the march. In 1991, a group of black teenagers was denied service at a Denny's Restaurant in San Jose, California. The students filed a lawsuit against Denny's that turned up hundreds of similar complaints against the restaurant chain, including minimum-purchase requirements, back-room seating, and disrespectful service directed at African Americans. Investigators discovered that the chain had instructed restaurant managers to discriminate against "A-A's", the in-house code for African Americans, and to try to limit the number of black customers. Responding to pressure, in 1994 Denny's overhauled its management-training policies, hired more black managers, and offered franchises to blacks; the chain also paid $46 million in compensation to the 4,300 customers who had experienced racial discrimination in Denny's restaurants.

By speaking out, the San Jose teenagers thus set an example that proved racial bias would not be tolerated. "We have to come to grips with the fact that racism does exist and not be so quick to try to rationalize it away or justify it, but to accept the fact that it's there and begin to do something about it," said Charles Moody, senior Vice President for Minority Affairs at the University of Michigan and founder of the National Alliance of Black School Educators. "I think people as individuals can do something about it by looking at themselves and trying to change that part of the institution or community that they have control over."

In addition to racial discrimination, there are pressing economic and social problems that continue to affect black communities. There is a disparity between the health of the black and white American populations. Black infants are twice as likely to die as are white infants, because black women receive early prenatal care far less frequently than do white women. In New York and New Jersey, AIDS is now the leading cause of death among African Americans between the ages of 15 and 44, and the Centers for Disease Control and Prevention has called the AIDS epidemic a major threat to African-American health.

Former secretary of Health and Human Services Louis Sullivan, himself an African American, believes that the nation needs to focus on such critical areas as the prevention of AIDS, homicides, and suicides. The problems of drug use, gangs, and crime also need to be addressed as the end of the 20th century approaches.

Many prominent African Americans have come forward with their opinions on what is needed to solve the nation's racial problems and close the gaps between the black and white populations. Mary Frances Berry, for example, former assistant secretary for education and also former civil rights commissioner, sees the need for a multipronged approach to the problems facing black Americans today:

> People say, 'Well, we should have self-help.' Somebody else says, 'Well, no, we don't need self help. What we should have is civil rights enforcement.' And somebody else says, 'We need more government,' or 'No, we need private sector.' You have to have all of those things: private sector, government, self-help, motivation, civil rights enforcement. All these can be put together as a strategy to try to do something about the people's problems. And there's a role for every kind of institution. Individuals, churches, community groups, have to motivate people. The government has to use tax money wisely and make good policy decisions and enforce civil rights. The private sector has to use its resources and its money. Police need to make neighborhoods safe. Everybody's got a role to play.

The problems facing African Americans today remain significant. But, in the words of former Los Angeles gang member Charles Rachal, who left the Million Man March with renewed enthusiasm for his community work, "This is for real and we are going to see it through. People will be surprised at how quickly we put things into place."

FURTHER READING

Barker, Lucius J., and Mack H. Jones. *African-Americans and the American Political System*. 3rd ed. New Jersey: Prentice Hall, 1994.

Carson, Claiborne, et al., eds. *The Eyes on the Prize Civil Rights Reader*. New York: Penguin Books, 1991.

Carter, Stephen. *Reflections of an Affirmative-Action Baby*. New York: Harper Collins, 1991.

Conti, Joseph G., and Brad Stetson. *Challenging the Civil Rights Establishment: Profiles of a New Black Vanguard*. London: Praeger, 1993.

Cowan, Tom, and Jack McGuire. *The Timelines of African-American History*. New York: Penguin Books, 1994.

Hampton, Henry, and Steve Fayer. *Voices of Freedom*. New York: Bantam, 1990.

Hanmer, Trudy. *Affirmative Action: Opportunity For All?* New Jersey: Enslow, 1993.

Hornsby, Alton, Jr. *Milestones in Twentieth Century Black American History*. Detroit: Visible Ink Press, 1993.

Jennings, James. *The Politics of Black Empowerment: The Transformation of Black Activism in Urban America*. Detroit: Wayne State University Press, 1992.

Lupo, Alan. *Liberty's Chosen Home: The Politics of Violence in Boston*. Boston: Little, Brown, and Co., 1977.

Lusane, Clarence. *African Americans at the Crossroads*. Boston: South End Press, 1994.

Malloy, Ione. *Southie Won't Go: A Teacher's Diary of the Desegregation of South Boston High School*. Chicago: University of Illinois Press, 1986.

Rose, Tricia. *Black Noise*. Middletown, CT: Wesleyan University Press, 1994.

Salak, John. *The L.A. Riots*. Brookfield, CT: Millbrook Press, 1993.

Stanley, Lawrence, ed. *Rap: The Lyrics*. New York: Penguin, 1992.

West, Cornell. *Race Matters*. Boston: Beacon Press, 1993.

Wilkinson, J. Howie III. *From Brown to Bakke*. New York: Oxford University Press, 1984.

INDEX

PICTURE CREDITS

Every effort has been made to contact the copyright owners of photographs and illustrations used in this book. In the event that the holder of a copyright has not heard from us, he or she should contact Chelsea House Publishers.

page

2: UPI/Bettmann
14-15: AP/Wide World Photos
17: The Bettmann Archive
20: UPI/Corbis-Bettmann
23: UPI/Bettmann Newsphotos
24-24: AP/Wide World Photos
28-29: UPI/Bettmann
32-33: UPI/Bettmann Newsphotos
35: AP/Wide World Photos
36: UPI/Corbis-Bettmann
39: UPI/Corbis-Bettmann
42-43: AP/Wide World Photos
45: AP/Wide World Photos
49: UPI/Bettmann
50: UPI/Bettmann Newsphotos
53: UPI/Bettmann
56-57: UPI/Bettmann
59: UPI/Bettmann
60: UPI/Bettmann
65: UPI/Bettmann
66: UPI/Bettmann
69: Reuters/Bettmann
72-73: Newsweek/Bernard Gotfryd
75: Photofest
76: Archive Photos
79: Photofest
80: Photofest
83: Reuters/Bettmann
86-87: Reuters/Corbis-Bettmann
88: UPI/Corbis-Bettmann
90-91: UPI/Corbis-Bettmann
96: Reuters/Corbis-Bettmann
99: Reuters/Corbis-Bettmann
102-103: Archive Photos
105: AP/Wide World Photos
106: AP/Wide World Photos
109: AP/Wide World Photos

MARY HULL holds a B.A. in history from Brown University. She is a freelance writer and the author of several histories for young adult readers. In recent years she has received a grant from the National Endowment for the Humanities, written about the travels of Marco Polo, and studied with the School for International Training in Kenya.

CLAYBORNE CARSON, senior consulting editor of the MILESTONES IN BLACK AMERICAN HISTORY series, is a professor of history at Stanford University. His first book, *In Struggle: SNCC and the Black Awakening of the 1960s* (1981), won the Frederick Jackson Turner Prize of the Organization of American Historians. He is the director of the Martin Luther King, Jr., Papers Project, which will publish 12 volumes of King's writings.

DARLENE CLARK HINE, senior consulting editor of the MILESTONES IN BLACK AMERICAN HISTORY series, is the John A. Hannah Professor of American History at Michigan State University. She is the author of numerous books and articles on black women's history, as well as the editor of the two-volume *Black Women in America: An Historical Encyclopedia* (1993). Her most recent work is a collection of essays entitled *Hine Sight: Black Women and the Re-Construction of American History.*